ANGELS
WHO ARE THEY?

By

Dennis H. Helton

Angels, Who Are They?

Address All Inquiries To:
THE OLD PATHS PUBLICATIONS, Inc.
142 Gold Flume Way
Cleveland, Georgia, U.S.A.

Web: www.theoldpathspublications.com
E-mail: TOP@theoldpathspublications.com

DEDICATION

To H.D. and Patricia Williams, Directors at TOP Publications, for the sacrificial giving of their time and valuable expertise in taking this book, *Angels, Who Are They?* through the process of publishing.

ACKNOWLEDGMENTS FOR THIS WORK

This writing of this paper was prompted by three Christian brethren:

- **Perry Giles** (who gave this novice-writer a book that further piqued his latent interest of angels)

- **Owen Roberson** (who is not blown about by every wind of doctrine)

- **Steve Morris** (who demonstrates genuine interest in Bible truths)

PREFACE

Angels – Who Are They? by Dennis H. Helton is a much needed book! Why? Because the "angelic theology" being promoted today is wildly unbiblical. This book is a valuable tool revealing the truth about angels and exposing what I call the "Celestial Quackery" of our day.

As I went through the book, I would characterize the first half as <u>a biblical answer book about angels</u>: How old are angels? What do men and angels have in common? Do angels have wings? What are the different kinds of angels? Are angels sexless? Do Christians become angels when they die? Do angels appear today? These are just some of the questions posed and answered. I especially appreciated the sections on the characteristics of Angels and the section where Brother Helton exposes the false teaching about angels in Mormonism, Islam, Catholicism and Theosophy.

The second half of the book was thought-provoking. It tackled the controversial interpretations of **Genesis 6:1-8** concerning – **Who are the sons of God?** The author characterizes the different positions for your evaluation.

Angels – Who Are They? is a fascinating book. It exposes the errors about angels and reinforces the truth about angels. It is worth your time and attention.

> *Psalms 34:7 The angel of the LORD encampeth round about them that fear him, and delivereth them.*

Dr. David L. Brown, Ph.D., Pastor
First Baptist Church, Oak Creek, WI

4

TABLE OF CONTENTS

PART I

WHO ARE THE ANGELS?

Angels are supernatural creatures of the *Spirit World* who are created above man's terrestrial world of natural order. Angels were created by God for His own purpose and pleasure.

There are both good angels and fallen bad angels

There is but a step from the natural world of man to the celestial spirit world of the angels. The veil of flesh is the separator. The angels of the spirit world (*both good and bad*) are mighty in strength.

The writer believes (or speculates) that perhaps the word "angels" may be a generic title that includes all of the various supernatural beings (Viz., Cherubim; Seraphim; spirits; demons; seducing spirits; Michael the archangel; Gabriel (the angel announcer from God to man; et al).

- Angels were present at Creation (Job 38:4-7)
- Angels are ministering spirits [servants] to the heirs of salvation [saved people] - (Hebrews 1:4).
- Angels are beings of great wisdom, desiring to know all things that are in the earth (2 Samuel 14:20; I Peter 1:12).
- Angels are beings of great strength - (Psalms 103:20).
- Angels serve as guardians - (Psalms 34:7; 91:11; Matthew 18:10).
- Angels can travel [fly] at great speed - (Daniel 9:21).
- Angels are an innumerable company - (Hebrews 12:22; Revelation 5:11).

- Angels are involved in many providential miracles of God - (Daniel 6:22).
- Angels accompany each believer at death into the presence of the Lord – (Luke 16:22; 2 Corinthians 5:8).
- Angels (some}became demons (Revelation 12:3, 4, 9)
- Jesus could have called twelve legions of angels (Matthew 26:53)
- We shall judge angels (I Corinthians 6:3)
- Man/humanity was made a little lower than the angels (Psalms 8:4, 5)
- Angels desire to look into salvation (I Peter 1:12)
- Angels are associated with the "Chariots of God" (Psalms 68:17)

Certain angelic beings are called "watchers" (Daniel 4:13, 17, 23) and observe human events. Paul said that he and the other apostles had been made a spectacle unto the world and to angels, and to men (I Corinthians 4:9). We can be sure that Christians (especially Christian leaders) are on the world stage being carefully watched by a cloud of great witnesses (Hebrews 12:1). The angels desire to look into the things here upon earth - (I Peter 1:12).This cloud of great witnesses (huge audience) undoubtedly includes both men and angels. It is interesting to note that Christian women are cautioned to maintain a covering on their head because of the angels - (I Corinthians 11:10).

Do Angels Have Wings?

The good angels (unfallen angels) have appeared on earth many times in the likeness of men without wings. We know that some angels have four wings, some six wings, and some possibly with two wings (as seen in the Holy of Holies within the Temple (I Kings 6:23-27). Angels may include separate forms of celestial beings as described by, wings, rings full of eyes, four faces, and a wheel within a wheel (Ezekiel 1:5-24), and even chariots of God (Psalms 68:17). They all are supernatural creations of God.

The angels of God are fascinating and mysterious creatures. They are prominent in Scriptures and mentioned about 273 times from Genesis to Revelation. They are created *celestial* spirit-beings and unlike created *terrestrial* men in many ways (Psalms 8:5; Hebrews 2:7; I Corinthians 15:39-40).

The Sadducees of the Jewish religious sect did not believe in angels (Acts 23:8). Many religious modernists today deny the existence of angels and relegate them to Babylonian and Persian myths. Of course, these religious agnostics (naturalists) are of the same vein of those who deny the miraculous and supernatural spirit world.

Mythologies of pagan nations picture angels as gods who convey messages from gods to men. The heathen called these spirit creatures: gods, fauns, nymphs, naiads, genii, semi-gods, and today, avatars. Actually, angels are one-way messengers, from God to man but not from man to God. Again, angels are created celestial beings with far superior powers above men (2 Peter 2:11).Man in his natural state is made a little lower than angels - (Psalms 8:5; Hebrews 2:7).

The writer believes that man, in his redeemed state (of a glorified body), may have equal or greater authority than angels (I Corinthians 6:3), simply because he (man) is created in the image of God; it is not said that angels were created in the image of God. Christ died for man which makes man very special to God. Jesus did not die that angels may have redemption after a fall; when angels fall, they are without excuse and without redemption, having been in the very presence of God and therefore totally without excuse. Man, being created in God's image, makes him a special

Creature of Redemption. The very fact that Jesus chose to enter the human race and become a man also speaks of God's special affection to man. When we see Christ we shall be like Him – (I John 3:2). Seeing as how we are to be like Christ (in His glorious fashion), we certainly will be greatly blessed of God. Other than man, it is not said of any other entity of God's Creation that it or he was made in the image of God.

> *I Corinthians 6:2-3: Do ye not know that the saints shall judge the world? And if the world shall be judged by you, are ye unworthy to judge the smallest matters? Know ye not that* **we (believers) shall judge angels?** *How much more things that pertain to this life?*

-Of course, we will not judge *fallen angels* in the matter of going to Hell. It is obvious from *I Corinthians chapter 6* that believers will judge *good angels* in some matters concerning their affairs.

Do Christians Become Angels When They Die?

Man does **not** become an angel when he dies. Angels are forever distinct from human beings. Angels never die; however death is appointed for man upon earth (Hebrews 9:27).

Again, the writer believes that redeemed man (in his glorified state) is destined for great things in the Kingdom of God:

   a) Man was originally created in the image of God (that image being marred by sin); nowhere are we told that angels are created in God's image.

   b) Men (not angels) are redeemed by the shed blood of Jesus Christ

10

c) Man's glorified body will be like unto Christ's body (I John 3:2).

d) Scriptures say that believers in Christ will judge angels (I Corinthians 6:2, 3)

How Old Are Angels?

We are not told the age of angels, although their age may be implied. It appears that God created angels before He created man because "Morning stars" and "sons of God" were present at the beginning of the Six-Day Creation Week (when God laid the foundation of the earth - (Job 38:4-7). The morning stars sang together, and all the sons of God shouted for joy. It also appears that these sons of God and morning stars were angels; men had not yet been created at this time. One Bible scholar suggests that angels may have been created on the first day of Creation right after the terrestrial universe was framed. Dr. Henry M. Morris says that angels were probably created on the first day of creation (there is no express statement of the time of the angel's creation).This writer believes that angels may have been created in eternity past before the 6-Day creation week of energy, space, matter, and measurable time (perhaps angels may not have been part of the 6-Day terrestrial creation). If angels had been created during the creation week, it would appear that it would have been stated; however, there is no direct statement that they were created during the 6-Day creation week. Again, this writer does not believe that the created angels were part of the 6-Day creation of earth, planets, stars, animals, the vegetable kingdom and man (the Bible is silent about any two creations).Of course, the writer is merely speculating on of the age of angels. Since angels do not die, it is reasonable to assume that angels may have been a creation of the "celestial" universe of God separate from of the creation of the time/space/energy creation of the "terrestrial" universe of God? Certainly, we must be careful

11

not to add to the Word of God. Again the writer is merely speculating upon the age of the angels.

Although, angels have great power above man, in the absolute sense, they are finite (limited) beings like you and me when compared to God.

When compared to our Creator. Angels of the OT are referred to as **sons of God** (Job 1:6-7; 2:1; 38:43, 7; Psalms 89:6). If the sons of God were part of creation and sang together at the creation, they had to have been created before the creation week of about 6,000 years ago. The consensus (opinion of most) of most Bible students and scholars is that the angels were created immediately before the creation of man.

Dr. Henry M. Morris says that according to Hebrew poetic parallelism, the morning stars and sons of God are the same as angels and likewise the singing and shouting for joy, the same - (Job 38:7).

Is It *possible* (?) that those sons of God in the controversial text of Genesis chapter six (see Part II of this writing), were also angels? Some speculate that these fallen angels are disembodied demonic spirits! Perhaps that may be true for some of the rebellious angels! It also appears that angels are sometimes referred to as "stars" in Revelation 12:4. It is the opinion of the writer that both morning stars and sons of God were angels who were present when God laid the foundation of the earth and rejoiced - (Job 38:4, 7). One writer stated that the Sons of God were believers who had died and were in Paradise, therefore able to observe Creation. However, man had not yet been created.

It is to be noted that while angels are called the sons of God, they are never called "the sons of the Lord." **A. C. Gaebelein** says, "It is in the Hebrew always *Bnai Elohim* (Elohim is God's name as Creator) and never *Bnai Jehovah* (Bnai is the Hebrew for sons). *Bnai Jehovah* are sinners redeemed and brought in the filial relationship by redemption. *Bnai Elohim* are unfallen beings, sons of God by creation. The angels are the sons of God first in creation, acknowledging that they rejoiced in it;" sinners saved by grace are the sons of God in the "new creation."

(**NOTE:** For a fair balance, the writer quotes another Christian writer's comment on this subject. He believes that A. C. Gaebelein's claim [that the giants referred to in *Genesis 6:4* were Nephilim, meaning "fallen ones"] is heresy — *The Perilous Times*, March/April 2007, p. 4.)

Are All Celestial Beings Angels?

Good question! According to Strong's Concordance, the word "angel" in the Old Testament is from the Hebrew word, "malak" (mal-awk'), and in the NT, from the Greek word, "aggelos" (ang' el-os). Again, the writer thinks that perhaps (?) the word "angel" may be a generic term that includes various kinds of created celestial beings. Cherubim have four wings (yet the cherubim of image work in Solomon's Temple appear to have only two wings (I Kings 8:6-7; 2 Chronicles 3:13; 5:8), and the Seraphim have six wings. This appears to suggest that the Cherubim, Seraphim, and the Four Living Creatures of Ezekiel may all be angels of different orders in certain aspects. The Cherubim with four wings and the Four Living Creatures with four faces appear to be one and the same (Ezekiel 10:5, 8, 12, 16, 19, 21). Perhaps the four faces allude to four orders of Cherubim. It is said of them that they had the likeness of Four Living Creatures, the likeness of a man, a lion, an ox, an eagle (Ezekiel 1:5-10), or else each one had four faces, left side, right side, front, and back (Ezekiel 1:10). These angelic creatures also are associated with fiery chariots described as it were, "a wheel in the middle of a wheel" (Ezekiel 1:16) and their speed as lightning (Ezekiel 1:14).

13

Some have even suggested that this is an explanation of the mysterious flying saucers and UFOs.

Cherubim: from the Hebrew root meaning to "grasp, hold, seize, or apprehend."

Cherubim are called "chariots of fire" in Psalms 68:17.

Seraphim: from the Hebrew root, seraph, meaning "to burn or shining ones; Hence the word Seraphim means "burning ones."

Seraphim are called a flame of fire in Psalms 104:4.

Although the Seraphim have six wings (Isaiah 6:2) and four faces and the Cherubim have four wings (or two), when angels appeared to men on earth (Hebrews 13:2), there is no mention made of wings. This 'may' even suggest another form of angels that are different from the Cherubim, Seraphim, and the four living creatures of Ezekiel (Perhaps, the **wingless** appearance of angels in the form of men is why some Bible commentators mistakenly teach that angels do not have wings). Many times in the Bible, angels were mistaken for mortal men. Even now, angels may be seen on earth and mistaken for men. Even when angels appeared to man in a dazzling, brilliant state, there is no mention made of wings. If angels manifested themselves with wings, they would not be mistaken for mere men, in both the OT and the NT. Again, the various descriptions of these marvelous angelic creatures support the idea that the word "angel" may be a generic title for all of the *celestial* creatures of God. Lucifer was a Cherub and Cherubim (Cherubim: plural for Cherub) have four wings (maybe some had two wings as the Cherubim over the Mercy Seat in the Holy of Holies). Perhaps Michael, Gabriel, and Lucifer were of an order of Cherubim that do not have wings. Although the writer does not believe that angels have to rely upon wings in order to fly through space, we are told in Isaiah 6:2 that the seraphim flew with two of his six wings, covered his face with two wings, and covered his feet with two wings. Lucifer is alluded to as the anointed Cherub (Ezekiel 28:14), and we know that Cherubim have been described as having four wings. If Michael and Gabriel are of the same order of Cherubim, they too would have four wings. In all four Gospel accounts, angels (without names) are seen at the tomb of Christ after His resurrection and there is no mention of them having wings (some even think that the two angels at Christ's tomb may have been Moses and Elijah in a glorified state who were with Christ when he was transfigured; others think the two angels may have been Elijah and Enoch who were translated without seeing death).

- -John says "two angels in white" (John 2:12).
- -Luke says, "two men in shining garments" (Luke 24:4).
- -Mark says, "a young man...clothed in a long white garment" (Mark 16:5).
- -Matthew says, "the angel of the Lord descended from heaven, and came and rolled back the stone from the door, and sat upon it. His countenance was like lightning, and his raiment white as snow:" (Matthew 28:2, 3).

Can Angels Be Numbered?

The angels are **innumerable** (Hebrews 12:22), but strangely to us (but not to God), only three of them are given names in the Bible, Michael, Gabriel, and Lucifer.

*Hebrews 13:2: Be not forgetful to entertain strangers: for thereby some have entertained **angels unawares**.*

There are occasions in the Bible when angels, attired in white and dazzling light, appeared in the presence of men and women. This had a frightening effect upon the beholder. As already stated, some Bible commentators say that angels do not have wings, but again, Seraphim and Cherubim certainly do, especially in their celestial realm. Again, it is apparent that some angels are able to appear on earth as men without wings.

What Do Angels Resemble?

Archaeologists have discovered in ancient near eastern iconography and architecture cherubim like figures that resemble biblical angelic creatures. Cherubim are depicted as: creatures part human, part animal; winged-humans; composites of lions and humans (sphinxes), winged bulls and humans; composites of birds and humans (griffins). We have various descriptions of angelic creatures in the book of Ezekiel. Of course, when angels appeared to men, they appeared in the likeness of men.

It appears to this writer that angels are also called, "chariots of God" (Psalms 68:17).

If UFOs are genuine sightings. this would be my answer for some UFO existence.

According to Randall Price (university professor, writer, and world-renown archaeologist), Ancient Near Eastern architecture depicts cherubim as....

- ✓ creatures that are part human and part animal

- ✓ in Sumer, figures of winged humans

- ✓ in Egypt, Syria, and Israel, winged humans or composites of lions and humans (sphinxes)

- ✓ in Assyria and Babylon, composites of winged bulls and humans

- ✓ In Greece, composites of birds and humans (griffins)

Price comments that the human part may suggests human intellect and emotion, while the winged-animal part may represent power and speed. Combined, the traits present a creature of an order above any earthy creation—the angelic. Local pagan mythology likely influenced the images.

Three Angels Named

It is mystifying to us (limited mortal thinking) that though there are myriads (countless; innumerable; indefinite large numbers) of angels, and yet we are only given the names of these three, **Michael**, **Gabriel**, and **Lucifer** (probably all three of the order of the cherubim). The king of Tyrus (Ezekiel 28:12-15) appears to be a "type" of fallen Lucifer who is called a cherub (single case for plural cherubim).

Michael

Michael: means, "Who is like God," and appears to be associated with war and conflicts. In Revelation 12:7, he is seen in command of the angelic army of Heaven. Michael is the chief commander of the host of heaven. He has something to do with the resurrection mentioned in Daniel 12:1-2, and he contested with the Devil over the body of Moses (Jude 9).He is mentioned three times in Daniel (Daniel 10:13, 21; 12:1) and is called a prince who stands for Daniel's people (the Jews).Although many generally consider all three angels (Michael, Gabriel, and Lucifer) "archangels," only Michael is specifically titled as an archangel in Scriptures. The voice of the Archangel will be heard when the dead in Christ shall rise (I Thessalonians 4:16).

Gabriel

Gabriel: means, "The Mighty One" and is mentioned by name four times, in *Daniel* twice (*Daniel 8:16; 9:21-27*), and in Luke twice (*Luke 1:19, 26, 27*).He appears to be associated with the redemptive work of God, and as a messenger. Gabriel said of himself to Zacharias, "I am Gabriel that Stand in the Presence of God. "It was Gabriel that gave the great announcement of the birth of Christ (*Luke 1:31-33*).Probably, the angelic host watched for this great event for 4,000 years and greatly rejoiced when Christ was born.

Lucifer

Lucifer: means, "the shining one," and not, "Morning Star" (which also shines). It is erroneously translated (or paraphrased) as morning star in some English "New Age Bibles." Lucifer was called the anointed Cherub that covereth in Ezekiel 28:10. The word "Lucifer" (son of the morning) is taken from the Jerome's Vulgate Bible which translated the Hebrew word "Helel" with the Latin Lucifer, light-bearer. It appears that the rebellious "king of Tyrus" is a type of Lucifer, the light-bearer (Ezekiel 28). Iniquity was in Lucifer, and he became a rebel (Ezekiel 28:12-15) who fell by pride, exalting himself (Isaiah 14:13, 14). Some Bible commentators think that Lucifer may have been the guardian or protector of the throne of God. Perhaps it would be fair to say that he is the source of universal rebellion. Lucifer has been deposed and Scripture calls him now by numerous titles (Viz., the Prince of this world; the devil; that old serpent; Satan; the god of this age; et al). Presently, Satan does not have a fixed habitation and is a wandering star in the heavens. In First Peter, we are warned about the prowling of Satan and his evil intentions:

*I Peter 5:8-9: Be sober, be vigilant; because your adversary **the devil**, as a roaring lion,*

walketh about, seeking whom he may devour:
Whom resist stedfast in the faith, knowing
that the same afflictions are accomplished in
your brethren that are in the world.

Satan's Great Delusion

One of Satan's best delusions is to convince the world of his "non-existence." The only true authority concerning the existence of Satan is the Bible and it reveals his wicked agenda (the opinions of wicked men do not count). Today, religious liberals, libertines (freethinkers), evolutionists, and atheists, are Satan's intellectual pawns.

Satan is not presently imprisoned and has great liberty in our world (I Peter 5:8). Remember that God allowed Satan much latitude concerning Job's trial. In the NT, Satan even dared to "test" Jesus. Of course, Jesus could only be tested and not "tempted" with sin because in Him (Jesus) was no sin. Jesus was God in the flesh upon earth (Galatians 4:4), and is forever God in His celestial body of unknown substance.

Concerning pride, we all would do well to reflect upon the failure of Peter's boasting lest we should be tempted to be lifted up in spiritual pride.

Is There a 4th Angel Named Palmoni?

Some members of the false religion of Mormonism teach that a "certain saint" named *Palmoni* was an angel that has been mistakenly overlooked by both students and scholars of the Bible. The writer investigated and found nothing to substantiate this false claim. (Palmoni: alleged compound name of the two words, Peloni and Almoni).

*Daniel 8:13: Then I heard **one saint** speaking, and another saint said unto that **certain saint** which spake, How long shall be the vision concerning the daily sacrifice, and the transgression of desolation, to give both the sanctuary and the host to be trodden under foot?*

In this verse, it is alleged by some that the "saints" mentioned here are angels, not men.

- The Hebrew word "certain" is Strong's #6422 which is palmoniy (pal-mo-nee')

- The Hebrew word for "angel" is Strongs's # 4397, which is malak (mnal-awk')

- The Hebrew word for "saint" is Strong's #6918, which is qadosh (kaw-doshe').

- Angels are never called saints; saints are earth men who have been redeemed.

This appears to be one redeemed saint speaking to another redeemed saint whether in a body or in a spirit form. Again, while it may appear to some that the saints in this context are angels, the writer cannot recall an angel ever being called a **saint** in the Scriptures. Saints are people who have been redeemed by the blood of the Lamb; angels have not been redeemed by the blood of the Lamb"…which things the angels desire to look into" (I Peter 1:12).

*Romans 1:7: "To all that be in Rome, beloved of God, called to be **saints**…"*

*I Corinthians 1:2: "Unto the church of God which is at Corinth, to them that are sanctified in Christ Jesus, called to be **saints**…"*

*I Corinthians 1:1: "...with all the **saints** which are in all Achaia."*

*Ephesians 1:1: "...to the **saints** which are at Ephesus..."*

*Philippians 1:1: "...to all the **saints** in Christ Jesus which are at Philippi...'*

Of course, the word "angel" **is** used in a figurative sense **as** in the book of Revelation, when addressing the messengers to the seven churches, but this does not mean that the pastors, elders, and spiritual leaders were literally angels. The angels were messengers to the seven representative churches. God does not use angels to preach the Gospel to the churches; God uses men (saints) to preach the gospel to other men.

The apostle Paul symbolically equates the kindness shown unto him by the saints of Galatia as "...received me **as** an angel of God..." (Galatians 4:14).

Who Are the Angels of World Religions? Some false prophets (Viz., Islam's Muhammad, Mormonism's Joseph Smith; Catholicism's counterfeit Mary; et al) attribute their religious beginning or guidance to an angel. In this way, they desire to convince others of their "alleged" divine authority. **Angels have never been authorized to establish any *true* religion.**

The Mormon angel

The "alleged" angel, called Moroni of the Mormon cult-religion, is not a messenger of God, but a fallen demon spirit. According to Mormon doctrine, this "so-called" angel gave Joseph Smith gold plates from which the Book of Mormon was translated. The Book of Mormon is "another gospel" that true believers are admonished to avoid – (Galatians 1:8). Mormons argue that God the Father and Jesus Christ appeared in dramatic form to Joseph Smith in

21

1820. Smith believed that he received revelations from God, Jesus, and many spirits of the dead, such as Peter, James, John the Baptist, and others.

The apostle Paul says that anyone preaching any other gospel, **even by an angel**, should be cursed. This certainly includes the "another-gospel" of Joseph Smith's fallen Moroni angel.

> *Galatians 1:6-9: I marvel that ye are so soon removed from Him that called you into the grace of Christ unto **another gospel**: Which is not another; but there be some that trouble you, and would **pervert the gospel of Christ**. But though we, **or an angel** from heaven, preach **any other gospel** unto you than that which we have preached unto you, **let him be accursed**. As we said before, so say I now again, if any man preach any other gospel unto you that that ye have received, **let him be accursed**.*

Mormonism says:

- -God the Father was once a man
- -God and his wife have physical bodies
- -Jesus was created as a spirit child
- -Jesus was the brother of Lucifer
- -Jesus received a body through sexual union between Elohim and Mary
- -Jesus and His death on the cross do not fully atone for sin
- o -Only the "works" of Mormon teaching and Mormon membership can give eternal life
- -Worthy men may one day become gods.
- -Mormonism says it is Christian

(*The Voice in the Wilderness*, p. 6, January/February 2008)

Paul pronounces a curse upon any substituted gospel, even by an angel. Paul calls any other gospel than the one that he himself preached, a false gospel. Paul also says, "Which is not another," meaning that there is **not** another true Gospel. There was only **one** true gospel and another true gospel would not follow.

Mormonism teaches the humongous lie that Jesus was the brother of Lucifer. Lucifer was created and being the brother of Lucifer would relegate Jesus to that of a created being, thereby denying the deity of Christ. Jesus has always been God from eternity past. Jesus is one with the Father (John 10:30).

(NOTE: The Bible did not come by an angel. God breathed out His original Word[s] to holy men of old by inspiration [2 Timothy 3:16; 2 Peter 1:19-21; Matthew 4:4]. God also preserved His Word forever [Psalms 12:7; 100:5; Isaiah 40:8; Matthew 4:4; 5:18; 24:35; Luke 4:4; I Peter 1:25]. The King James Version is a trustworthy, accurate English translation from the preserved copies of copies (apographs) from the original preserved manuscripts. The original Hebrew preserved manuscripts are the Hebrew Ben Chayyim. The original preserved Greek manuscripts are the Textus Receptus, Majority Text, Received Text, Beza's 5th Edition of 1598.

The Muslim angel(s)

Neither are Islam's phony angels and phony scriptures (Koran; Quran) from God. Can the reader guess the origin of the Islamic scriptures? Yes, another impersonator angel! Islam claims that *their* scriptures came from God through the angel Gabriel (Jibril). While Muhammad was in a cave in a lonely place in the mountains, he experienced visions of the angel Gabriel who commanded him to "Recite" in the name of the Lord. Actually the angel threatened to choke Muhammad if he did not write.

Of course, the Holy Spirit warns of the deception of wicked spirits (I John 4:1, 6) and guided Paul to alert true believers against the deceiving spirits claiming heavenly guidance (I John 4:1-6).Of course, most all of the phony sects and cults make claims to heavenly visions and guidance (as do some charismatics). They know that carnal man is far more prone to being influenced by claims of "so-called" divine manifestations and visions than to receiving the Word of God by faith alone.

Islam's four archangels:

1.) Jibril or Gabriel, the messenger of revelation --- much confused with the Holy Spirit

2.) Mika'il or Michael, the guardian of the Jews

3.) Israfil, the summoner to resurrection

4.) 'Izra'il, the messenger of death

According to Islam, between angels (created out of light), there is also a multitude of creatures called "jinn" that are created of smokeless flame. The jinn often appear as animals, reptiles, or in human form.

(Perhaps the fairy tale of the Arabian geni emerging in smoke by rubbing a magic lamp, originated from this fairy tale!)

The Catholic angel

Though they do not attribute the Scriptures to Mary, Roman Catholics do endorse numerous or "alleged" appearances (apparitions) of Mary in a mysterious spirit form.

The Catholic angel is believed to be Mary, the mother of Jesus. The "so-called" apparitions of Mary are demonic. The real Mary **would not appear** if she could and **could not if she would**. The writer does not put one stitch of confidence in the genuineness of apparitions of Mary. If images, apparitions, or spirits did appear as claimed, they are simply demonic spirits imitating an idol that millions bow before, adore, and even equate to divine status.

Some pray to a Mary, but it is not the Mary of the Bible. It is the wicked "queen of heaven" (Jeremiah 7:18; 44:17-19, 25). Easter or Astarte is known in the Bible as the "queen of heaven" (This pagan Mary has many names: Easter; Eastra; Ishtar; Ostara; Astarte; Ashtoreth; Diana; Isis; Athena; Europa; Minerva; Venus; Aphrodite). This female teutonic goddess of spring, was the goddess of love, fertility, and maternity for Phoenicians, Canaanites, Arameans, South Arabs, and Egyptians. Ishtar (Easter) was identified with the planet Venus. The Greeks called her Aphrodite and the Romans, Venus. As the Babylonian and Assyrian deity, Ishtar was also the goddess of war.

Sadly, even the wise King Solomon "un-wisely" went after Ashtoreth (I Kings 11:5, 33: II Kings 23:13; Jeremiah 7:18; 44:17-25).

The Roman Empire established Christianity as the only legal religion in the late fourth century (or about 325 AD).This involved the worship of a pagan goddess of Babylon addressed as, "The Holy Virgin," "The Virgin Mother," and "Queen of Heaven and Earth." Romans Christianized those titles by ascribing them to the virgin Mary and the Roman Church eventually adopted them. Many Catholics pray to Mary instead of praying to God. They claim to be merely *venerating* her but not worshipping her. A Catholic co-worker told this writer that they (Catholics) feel unworthy to approach God or Jesus directly and so they go through Mary as a "go-between." My Catholic friend went on to tell me that Mary had a lot of influence with Jesus and she could incline Jesus to give favor. The writer does not know if this is the true sentiment of all Catholics or not; however, this teaching does appear to be in accordance to Catholic teachings.

*I Timothy 2:5: For there is one God, and **one mediator between God and men**, the man **Christ Jesus**.*

There is no room in this verse for a preacher, priest, pope, cardinal, imam, guru, saint, caliphate, or Mary.

The virgin or Mother Goddess has perennially been the **tangible icon** through which that "nature god" has been addressed and venerated. An <u>engraving on a goddess icon</u> from ancient Egypt reads, *"I am all that has been, or that is, or that shall be"* - (Alexander Hislop, *The Two Babylons,* p. 77).

Madam Blavatsky States (of Theosophy)

Imprudent (*rash; without thought; indiscreet*) are the Christian theologians who have degraded them into Fallen Angels and now call them Satan and his demons. Is he not...Sanatsuyala, another name of **Mother**...the **Celestial Virgin--Mother of the Invisible Universe**, also called the Great Dragon- (H. P. Blavatsky, *The Secret Doctrine*, Vol. I, London: The Theosophical Publishing Society, 1893, pp. 495-496).

Theosophy: a religious set of occult beliefs rejecting Judeo-Christian revelation and often incorporating elements of Buddhism and Hinduism held to be based upon mystical insight or alleged superior speculation.

B.F. Westcott agrees with Blavatsky that visions of 'the virgin' are merely 'God' changing "form." (Westcott is the editor of the New Greek text underlying the NIV, NASB, RSV, ERV and most of the unreliable, New Age Bible versions.)

Reports of visions of *virgins* and apparitions of *Mary* are occurring worldwide and the title 'The Virgin' has been applied to the goddesses of...

- Canaanites -- Astarte and Ashtoreth

- Babylon -- Rhea or Semiramis and Baal or Bel (*Jeremiah 51:44*)

- Egyptians -- Isis (goddess mother), Horus (child)

- Hindus -- Isi, Kanyabava, Trigana

- Rome -- Venus (goddess), Jupiter (child), mother of Romulus and Remus)

- Greco-Roman goddesses -- Ceres, Hestis, Vesta, Diana, Artemis, Demeter, and Cybele

- China -- Shing Moo (Holy Mother)

- Greece -- Aphrodite, The Mediatrix

- India -- Devaki (goddess), Crishna (child)

- Ephesus -- Diana (the mother of gods identified with Semiramis)

- Scandinavia -- Disa (pictured with a child)

- Israel -- Ashtaroth (goddess), Baal (child) - *Judges 2:13*

- Africa -- the Great Mother and Child received divine honors

- Catholicism's Mary (not Mary, mother of Jesus, as claimed by the Catholic Church)

The Root of Mary worship

✓ Semiramis (sih MIHR uh mihs) was a mythical queen of Assyria who supposedly founded the ancient city of Babylon, and conquered Persia and Egypt.

✓ Herotus mentions a Semiramis who was queen of Babylon in the 700's B.C - *World Book Encyclopedia*, Volume 17, p.235, copyright 1980, USA.

✓ Semiramis became a goddess with many names: Baalti, (The Madonna), The Great Goddess Mother, Queen of Heaven, The Mediatrix, The Mother of Mankind, Astarte, etc.

✓ The Catholic Council of Chalcedon in AD 451 proclaimed Mary's **perpetual virginity.** This is strange considering Mary had other children (Matthew 12:46-47; 13:55; Mark 3:31; Luke 8:19-20; John 2:12; 7:5; Acts 1:14).

Alexander Hislop (almost 100 years ago) concluded that 'the Virgin' would be the "image of the beast" worshipped during the great tribulation (*The Two Babylons*, p. 263).

New Age writers concede that this 'virgin' is indeed the Great Dragon which Revelation 20:2 reveals to be Satan.

An Angel from Heaven

Again, Scriptures place a **curse** upon any imaginable being, even an angel from heaven that should preach any other Gospel than Jesus Christ. God's inspired Words were given to us through saved men only, not through impostor demonic entities.

*Galatians 1:8: But though we, or **an angel from heaven**, preach any other gospel unto* *you than that which we have preached unto you,* **let him be accursed***.*

Satan has energized his evil ministers to deceive:

2 Corinthians 11:13-15: For such are false apostles, deceitful workers, transforming themselves into the apostles or Christ. And no marvel; for **Satan himself is transformed into an angel of light***. Therefore* **it is no great thing if his ministers also be transformed as the ministers of righteousness***; whose end shall be according to their works.*

Why Do Some Claim that Jesus is a Created Angel?

ANSWER: **They are not of God.** They are of their father the devil (John 8:44).

Arianism [er'e an iz'am] is the doctrine of Arius, who taught that Jesus was not of the same substance as God, but a created being exalted above all other creatures.

I John 2:22-23: Who is a liar but he that denieth that Jesus is the Christ? **He is antichrist, that denieth the Father and the Son***. Whosoever denieth the Son, the same hath not the Father: but he that acknowledgeth the Son hath the Father also.*

John 8:24: I said therefore unto you, that ye shall die in your sins: for if ye believe not that I am he, ye shall **die in your sins***.*

See also I John 2:22-23; 4:1-3, 14-15; 5:1, 5, 10-11, 20; 2 John 7-9; John 1:1-3, 14, 34.

Jesus appeared repeatedly in the OT in the form of a man (or angel) in a pre-incarnate form (called a Theophany or Christophany: manifestation of Deity - Genesis 16:7).

Jesus was NOT created and is NOT an angel as some religious cult members claim (Viz., Jehovah's Witnesses; Mormonism; et al).

In a Jehovah's Witnesses' book, *Paradise Lost and Paradise Regained*, the writer claims that Jesus is made the brother of Michael the archangel. Mormonism claims that Jesus is the half-brother of Michael the archangel or the brother of Lucifer.

Jesus Is God and Never an Angel

The angel of Hebrew "Malach-Jehovah" is not a created being; He is un-created. It is Jehovah, the Lord, who revealed Himself at different times. Jesus appeared with the three Hebrew children in the fiery furnace. It was Jesus who wrestled with Jacob. It was Jesus who visited Abraham with two angels and all three appeared as ordinary men.

If Jesus was merely an angel and no more (angels are not worthy to die for sinners), man would be without a sacrifice for his sin. Man would be without God and without hope of reconciliation to God.

> *I John 2:22-23:* **Who is a liar but he that denieth that Jesus is the Christ?** *He is antichrist, that denieth the Father and the Son.*

> *I John 4:3, 15:* **And every spirit that confesseth not that Jesus Christ is come in the flesh is not of God:** *and* **this is that spirit of antichrist** *whereof ye have heard that it should come; and even now already is it in the world. Whosoever shall confesss that*

Jesus is the Son of God, God dwelleth in him, and he in God.

I John 5:1, 13: **Whosoever believeth that Jesus is the Christ is born of God:** *and every one that loveth Him that begat loveth Him also that is begotten of Him. These things have I written unto you that believe on the name of the Son of God; that ye may know that ye have eternal life, and that ye may believe on the name of the Son of God.*

2 John 7, 9: **For many deceivers are entered into the world, who confess not that Jesus Christ is come in the flesh.** *This is a deceiver and an antichrist. Whosoever transgresseth, and abideth not in the doctrine of Christ, hath not God.He that abideth in the doctrine of Christ, he hath both the Father and the Son.*

John 14:6: Jesus saith unto him (Thomas), I am the way, the truth, and the life: no man cometh unto the Father, but by Me.

John 8:24: I said therefore unto you, that ye shall die in your sins: **for if ye believe not that I am He, ye shall die in your sins.**

Are Angels Indirectly Referred to in Scriptures?

There are incidents in Scriptures where angels are not expressly stated though angels were obviously inferred. Elisha's servant was stricken with fear when he saw enemy military forces surrounding the city where they were residing, and Elisha's prayer to comfort him was answered at once. Scales were removed from the young man's eyes, and he saw the mountain full of horses and chariots of fire round about (the host of angels, Heaven's warriors) - 2 Kings 6:14-17.

In the book of Daniel, angels are revealed as "watchers" Daniel 4:13, 17, 23). Angels are referred to as "stars" (Jude 13; Revelation 9:1-2; 12:4, 7, 9).Men are sometimes called angels. The messengers (bishops; pastors; elders) to the Seven Churches in the Book of Revelation are called angels (Revelation 2:1, 8, 12, 18; 3:1, 7, 14).Even the pagan king, Achish, referred to David as "an angel of God" (I Samuel 29:9).Of course, this was figurative speech lauding David's personal attributes.

What Do Angels and Men Have in Common?

One outstanding aspect common to both angels and men is that they both have a *free will* (which contrasts with the false doctrine of **5-Point Hyper-Calvinism**). "Free will" is refuted by Hyper-Calvinists. How else could Lucifer have led astray the angels (perhaps a third of them – Revelation 12:4) if they did not have a free will to rebel?

God did not force angels to sin; if so, God would have sinned, and we know from Scriptures that God cannot sin. From Scriptures, it is evident that God has no pleasure in creating zombies or robots that have no will of their own. A forced will by God upon His creatures would not give Him pleasure knowing that the subjects did not really love Him, solely of their own volition (conscious deliberate choice) of a free will. God has chosen to give both angels and men a free will in choosing or rejecting Him. Of course, God can and has caused both men and devils to obey His will against their own when it pleased Him to accomplish a particular thing (Viz., Balaam's favorable prophecy of Israel; Caiaphas' prophecy of Messiah – John 11:49-52).

The time will come when all rebellious men and all rebellious angels will one day be cast into the eternal lake of fire (many are already in Hell). Presently, men have a day of grace when they may accept the Gospel call to salvation (2 Corinthians 6:2). **The fallen angels will never have a day of grace.** The rebellious angels are doomed and damned forever. Faith in God was *not* a prerequisite for them for they had the absolute **proof** of God's presence before them. Man must come to God by **faith** in Jesus Christ or else they are lost for eternity (John 14:6; I Timothy 2:5; Acts 4:12; Ephesians 2:8-9). Blessed are those who have not seen, yet believe.

Jesus did not lay hold of angels but of the seed of Abraham (Hebrews 2:16). the angels fell and Jesus let them go without hope or help. Christ never designed to be the Saviour of the fallen angels. As their tree fell, it must lie for all eternity; Christ did not assume the angel's nature.

Are Angels Sexless?

It does not appear that angels are sexless as some Bible commentators innocently, but erroneously teach. The writer thinks that most Bible commentators misunderstand Jesus' words in Luke's Gospel concerning the sex gender of angels.

> *Luke 20:35-36: But they (the redeemed from earth) which shall be accounted worthy to obtain that world, and the resurrection from the dead, **neither marry, nor are given in marriage:** Neither can they die any more: for they are **equal unto the angels**; and they are the children of God, being the children of the resurrection.*

Although many Bible scholars state that angels are sexless, the Scriptures nowhere substantiate such a claim. This opinion of sexlessness is assumed. In the context of Luke chapter 20, the relationship between men and women upon earth is compared to angels in the celestial realm (Heaven). Jesus **does say that angels do not marry in Heaven** (and presumably anywhere else). However, if angels were sexless or neuter gender, it would not be necessary to say they do not marry because that fact would be obvious (if angels were sexless). Since angels never die, they do not need to procreate themselves. Actually, because they do not die (Luke 20:36), Jesus could not take on a body of the substance of an angel. Jesus was made a little lower than the angels and took upon Himself the nature of man so that He could die for the sins of man. **Not only do angels not die, they don't get sick or even age**.

Some have thoughtlessly suggested that men may procreate in Heaven, but Jesus said that there are no marriages in Heaven and again there is no need for angels to procreate because they never die. Jesus said that the children of God are equal unto the angels in the resurrection from the dead – (Luke 20:35, 36.)

Angels Relegated To Male Gender

Often, we run across paintings of female angels, but female angels are nowhere alluded to in the Bible. The writer assumes that this is the reason that some writers call angels sexless. If angels were portrayed as both male and female, we might innocently, but **erroneously,** suppose that marriages between them might exist.

The angels mentioned all have masculine names; the pronouns in reference to angels are always masculine (**he**) – Matthew 28:2-4; 2 Samuel 24:16; I Chronicles 21:15; Acts 12:7; Revelation 22:8, 9. When angels appeared visibly to people upon earth, they always had the appearance of men, but never that of women (this does not fare well with the faulty biblical paintings of many artists). Angels of the Bible were limited to male gender, and that fact should shed a ray of light upon the *unenlightened* artists' portrayals of "baby" angels, "female" angels, and even 'long-haired" portrayals of Jesus.

Perhaps because the angels are identified in the male gender is one of the main reasons that God's **first** order of creation of humanity (Adam) was to be of male gender. The sons of God (presumably male angels) were present at Creation (Job 38:7).

Of course, all three members of the Godhead (Trinity) are referred to in the male gender, not a female gender as "she," or "her." Some New Age bibles (as one version of the NIV), that uses a female gender in reference to God, are being promoted by apostate theologians and liberals.

The male gender of angels is emphasized many times:

In Matthew 28:1-5, we have an **angel** identified as a young **man**. The Holy Spirit often calls angels **men** (Genesis 18:2; 19:1; Zechariah 1:10, 11; Luke 24:4; John 20:12; Acts 1:10; Mark 16:5).

- ✓ Cornelius perceived **an angel as a man** (Acts 10:30, 31).
- ✓ Even male sodomite homosexuals identified **angels as men** (Genesis 19:6-8).

Characteristics of Angels

➢ **Angels are holy:** Obviously, this refers to the "unfallen" angels (Revelation 14:10).

> **Angels were present at Creation:** Angels are older than anything we can see in earthly Creation. Job's presumptuous knowledge (or the lack of it) was chided by the Lord concerning Creation. Neither Job nor any of the OT saints, were present at Creation, but the morning stars (sons of God; angels) were (Job 38:1-7).

We are told in Revelation 12:3-4 that the dragon's tail "...drew the third part of the stars of heaven, and did cast them to the earth." The "stars of heaven" in this text appear to be in reference to the fallen angels who followed Satan in his rebellion against God.

> **Angels are not omnipresent:** They are unable to be everywhere at the same time.

> **Angels are not omniscient:** They do not know the day and hour of the Lord's Second Coming (Matthew 24:36). Angels do not fully understand the grace of God toward man, and desire to look into it (I Peter 1:12).

> **Angels are not omnipotent:** Angels have great power (2 Thessalonians 1:7) and strength (Psalms 103:20). An angel of the Lord smote 185,000 Assyrians in one night (2 Kings 19:35). Though angels are awesome and majestic, they are limited. Though the power of angels is staggering and they are able to unleash destruction exceeding any nuclear device of man (see the 7-Seals of Revelation), angels are impotent without God.

> **Angels do not marry in Heaven and cannot die (Luke 20:27-36):** Angels do not cut, bleed, and die. Angels know nothing of growing old and sickly. They know nothing of our afflictions in their life (Viz., pain; heart disease; cancer; diabetes; arthritis; high blood pressure; Alzheimer's disease; dementia; allergies; bronchitis; strokes; hearing loss; vision blindness; et al).

> ➤ **Angels are created spirit beings:** The nature of the angelic body is not revealed. We are not told of what substance or material their bodies consist. It does not appear that they breathe, have blood, and certainly do not consist of earth flesh (terrestrial).

> ➤ **Angels are God's ministering spirits**: Angels minister to the heirs of salvation (Hebrews 1:14). Angels may be ordered of God to assist our needs. However, they are not given the privilege of preaching the Gospel of Jesus Christ; that privilege is given exclusively to redeemed man.

> ➤ Angels run and return like a flash of lightning (Ezekiel 1:14). Seraphim means "burners."

> ➤ It appears that upon death, believers will be escorted to Heaven **by an angel** (Luke 16:22).

> ➤ **Angels were present at Mt. Sinai:** Angels were present at the giving of the Holy Law (Galatians 3:19; Acts 7:53; Deuteronomy 33:2).

> ➤ **Angels watch over God's children** (Matthew 18:10; Hebrews 1:14):

> ➤ **Angels do not accept worship:** The good (unfallen) angels reject worship from men; however, the desire of the antichrist person (a man indwelt by Satan) is for man to worship the Devil (Revelation 13).

> ➤ **Angels are innumerable** (Hebrews 12:22): Probably of the more than 250 times God calls Himself "The Lord of Hosts," meaning heavenly armies, it is speaking of angels as the host of God. Why would God create such a large number of angels when He certainly did not need so many of them? Of course, God created the angels for His own pleasure, but perhaps He also had a purpose for them with our interest in mind. There doesn't appear to be any reason to think that God has created any more angels than

at their beginning (created before man); neither does there appear to be any reduction of them (except the fallen ones). Since they do not die, we have as many today as we've ever had. Because the angels are innumerable, we could no more count them than we could count the stars.

➤ God's throne and the third Heaven is the angel's dwelling place. They will be a large part of our future environment. An angel (fallen Lucifer; the serpent; the devil) appeared in early "Creation" at the Garden of Eden. Cherubim were placed at the east of the garden with flaming swords to keep the way of the tree of life (Genesis 3:24).

➤ **Angels have appeared and do appear as ordinary men** (Hebrews 13:2).

➤ **Angels that sinned are cast down to Hell** (2 Peter 2:4; Jude 6): Of course, it appears that only "certain" angels of the total number that sinned were cast down to Hell (perhaps those of Genesis chapter 6). The Scriptures appear to imply that the total number of sinning angels with Satan's rebellion was one-third (Revelation 12:4).

➤ **Angels will administer judgments**: Angels have often ministered judgment to men upon earth and judgments will greatly escalate upon earth during Daniel's last half of the Seventh Week (a period of 3 ½ Years). This is referred to as The Great Tribulation, as seen under the 7-Seals in the Book of Revelation and Jeremiah 30:7.

➤ **Angels will be reapers:** Angels will gather up unbelievers (tares among the wheat) at the close of the age (Matthew 13:38-42). They will sever the wicked from the just in the end of the world – Matthew 13:49.

➤ **Angels rejoice:** Angels rejoice over one sinner that repenteth (Luke 15:10).

> ➢ **Michael the archangel:** Michael will prevail against the Devil (Revelation 12:7-9). Actually, Michael is the only angel specifically titled as an "archangel" (though Lucifer and Gabriel "may" have been).

➢ **Angels smote the Sodomites:** Angels foiled the perverted sexual advances of the sodomites with blindness - Genesis 19:11. (Modern sodomite euphemisms: homosexuals; lesbians; transgenders; gays; sads; LGBTs; queers)

➢ **Lucifer (now, "Satan"):** Lucifer was a high ranking anointed Cherub of great beauty before his fall (Ezekiel 28:13-19) and a perhaps a guardian of God's throne.

➢ **Satan, the fallen angel, the Devil:** With God's permission, the Devil tempted (tested) Jesus when He was weak and an hungred. This temptation (testing) was an outward tempting because Jesus could not be tempted from within for there was no sin in Him. "Jesus Was Without Sin And Is Forever Without Sin."

➢ **Angels ministered to Jesus:** Angels ministered to Jesus after His temptation (testing) of the Devil (Matthew 4:11).

➢ **Angels observed Jesus:** Angels observed Jesus' Life on earth. They saw His Birth, Sufferings, Death, Resurrection, and Ascension (I Timothy 3:16; Galatians 4:4).

➢ **Angel of the Lord:** An angel descended from heaven and rolled back the stone from the door of the sepulchre where Jesus had been entombed (Matthew 28:2-3).

Of course, this was not necessary in order for Jesus to exit the tomb but to let others enter the tomb. "He is not here: for He is risen, as He said…" (Matthew 28:6).

➢ **An angel:** An angel came at certain times to the pool Bethesda, agitating the waters so that healing powers were imparted – John 5:1-9.(Many psycho-critics and pseudo-fundamentalists attack this record and question its genuineness.)

➤ **Angels:** Myriads of angels (Myriad: 10,000 or any large indefinite number) join in the praise when the redeemed sing their song in Heaven, "...Thou art worthy to take the book, and to open the seals thereof, for thou wast slain, and hast redeemed us to God by thy blood out of every kindred, and tongue, and people, and nations" (Revelation 5:9)

➤ **An angel of the Lord**: An angel smote wicked Herod because Herod gave not the glory to God. Herod was eaten of worms (Acts 12:23).

➤ **Wicked angels:** It appears that Lucifer (the Serpent; the Devil) led astray one-third of the angels in Heaven (called "stars") in his rebellion – (Revelation 12:4, 7, 9; Jude 13).They left their first estate and will never be re-instated to it.

➤ **Pseudo-Angels:** We must not shape angels to suit our own fancy of thinking. Angels are incorrectly pictured in various forms (paintings, lapel pins, jewelry; china, figurines, art, etc.) as:

-chubby, pink-face babies with halos about their heads

-slender women with transparent wings

-men with long hair (resembling women), and so on.

Some angels are erroneously supposed by some to be deceased men (or women) that were transformed into an angel after death.

➤ **Chief fallen angel, Satan:** He loves to radiate and counterfeit the shining brilliance of **un**-fallen angels. He is not an angel of light (though Lucifer means "shining one") but masquerades as one (2 Corinthians 11:14).

➤ **Angel's influences:** They affect us to a greater reverence of God, but Christians are not to pray to them (nor pray to Mary and deceased saints). Angels are not to be worshipped! John fell down and was tempted to worship before the feet of an angel but the angel said unto him, **"See thou do it not...Worship God"** - (Revelation 22:8-9).Joseph, the foster-father of Jesus, as well as other believers, did not go into "angel-mania" from their supernatural encounters with angel messengers. How unlike the charismatic mystics of today! Angels cannot give our soul fulfillment.

➤ Angels are spirits and do not need food; yet they can assume bodily form (physical ?) and ingest food (Genesis 18;8; Hebrews 13:2).

Angels do not compare to Jesus:

God has highly exalted Jesus, and given Him a name which is above every name, that at the name of Jesus every knee should bow, of things in heaven, and things in earth, and things under the earth; And that every tongue should confess that Jesus Christ is Lord, to the glory of God the Father (Philippians 2:10-11).

Do Angels Appear Today?

There are limited reports in modern times of angels who are **seen** in a glorious form and other occasions where they were presumed to be ordinary men. The writer believes the scarcity of known angelic appearances is because God expects man to live by faith alone, and to trust in His Completed (plenary) Scriptures (Romans 1:17; 5:1; Hebrews 11:6), **The Word of God**.

Of course, this does not mean that angels are no longer active in the affairs of human experience and the service of God. In Bible times, God sometimes removed the scales from human eyes and people saw angels. The angels are still visitors to earth today and will have much authority during The Great Tribulation of the judgments of God upon earth. The writer believes that angels perform acts for people of God today upon earth. Probably the acts are done mostly "invisibly," but this does not rule out angels appearing as ordinary men. There are many claims, traditions, and legends that holy men and women were visited by angels; of course, no one can vouch for the genuineness of many of these claims. The writer definitely believes that angels are active in the affairs of men today, whether visibly or invisibly.

Today, we also have phony claims by phony religious leaders of being entertained in visions and dreams by angels and saints. Others lay claim of witnessing literal apparitions.

(**The Word of God:** God's name is to be praised; His name is holy and reverend, but God has magnified **His Word** above all His name – Psalms 138:2. We are to rejoice more in **The Word of God** rather than the appearance of an angel.)

> *Galatians 1:8: But though we, or **an angel** from heaven, preach any other gospel unto you than that which we have preached unto you, let him be accursed.*

> *Matthew 16:4: A wicked and adulterous generation seeketh after **a sign**; and there shall **no sign** be given unto it, **but the sign of the prophet Jonas**. And He left them, and departed.*

The writer has heard many stories of unusual events relating to the presence of angels, but doubts most of them. Many times people want to believe that they are witnesses to an astounding or unusual historical event (much like those who claim to have seen UFO's). Some people get a pleasant "rush" of some sort by daring to claim to have been a witness to a supernatural occurrence of a sensational level. Many times, explainable "unexplained phenomena" is mistaken for the supernatural. There are many false stories of angels entering the affairs of man; but most of these things cannot be easily verified, and usually there is only a lone witness to the incident.

It is the writer's belief that the reason that God does not allow angels to "visibly" adorn our world is because man is highly prone to cling to the excitement of the miraculous rather than living by faith (the unseen). God wants us to trust in His Word rather than rely upon supernatural proofs (remember doubting Thomas). In the past, God's Word was not complete and available to all; but now we have both Bible Testaments (OT & NT) in one canon of Scriptures for our learning and admonition. The most important message from God to man is the Gospel of His Son, Jesus Christ. God did not choose to allow angels to preach the Gospel; they have not been redeemed by Christ's shed blood. If any man or a mighty angel preaches any other Gospel than that of Christ, God has pronounced a curse upon them (Galatians 1:8)

Stories of Angels That Appear to Have Merit

◆ Several North Carolina preachers (and others) have told the rescue story of an eighteen-wheeler truck rapidly descending a steep incline in the North Carolina mountains. In spite of a rapid descent at an uncontrollable speed due to brake failure, the truck driver was able to maneuver the truck down the curvy, steep grade to a safe stop. Afterwards, an observer to the hair-raising event asked the truck driver a stunning question, "Who was that shining man on the front of your truck?" The truck driver replied that he did not see anyone! This story (?) has been around for a long time.

There have been other similar stories in other places and other times of "shining men" to the rescue.

◆ This writer's wife had a flat tire while driving through a dangerous neighborhood of our town late one evening near dark (with a small child). Of course, she was frightened, didn't know how to change to a spare tire, and was too afraid to try. The writer had previously warned her before about traveling this particularly unsafe route, especially at nighttime. She said, "Out of nowhere, a man appeared (not in dazzling, shining light) and immediately installed the spare tire." She offered him money, but he refused it. Before leaving the dangerous area, she looked around to thank him and offer to pay him, but he had **disappeared** from the scene about as suddenly as he had **appeared**. She swears to the story! Angel-man from heaven or "providentially sent" earth-man, it was still a God-send! (Of course, this was in the days long before cell phones and convenient means of communications).

◆ In New England in the early nineteenth century, a dying man sent for a certain circuit-riding preacher who was preaching less than a mile away. The preacher was ushered into a dimly lit room where the sick man lay in the throes of death. "Reverend," the dying man said hoarsely, "there is something I want you to know. Twelve years ago, you preached a meeting in the old church up on the ridge, west of here about seven miles." He sputtered and coughed: "Do you remember?" "Yes," the preacher answered, "I was in the service on your last night of the meeting. They collected a sizable offering for you. I watched you put the money in your saddlebag and ride away in the moonlight."

"You had made mention in the service what town you were riding to that night, so I got on my horse, took a short cut and laid in wait for you in the woods."

"I was going to rob you, Reverend. I saw you coming up the road in the moonlight. I was getting ready to jump out in front of you and take your money at gunpoint. Just before I made my move, you halted the horse and stepped down. Do you remember?"

"Yes I do," the preacher replied. "I had been having trouble with the cinch working loose and I stopped to tighten it."

Nodding his head slowly, the sick man said, "Yes. And I was getting ready to crack you over the head with my gun barrel when that man suddenly appeared and stood between you and me. Funny thing. You never seemed to notice him. You didn't even look up."

"I never saw him.'

"That's what I figgered. That's why I wanted to tell you about it. When I heard you were here in town, I wanted to tell you about it. Thought you ought to know. Somebody's sure watchin' out for you!"

With a strange light in his eyes, the preacher asked, "Sir, could you describe him?"

"Bout all I can tell you is that he was dressed in white clothing. Sure did glisten in the moonlight. He just stood in the road and looked my direction until you had ridden out of sight. Then, all of a sudden, he was gone!"

◆ A missionary family was laboring amongst a primitive tribe in Africa. The missionaries were fully aware of the danger of this particular tribe, but they trusted the Lord to protect them. After working with the natives for several years, they were finally able to win the tribal chief to Christ. Rejoicing in his newfound salvation, the chief asked the missionary to come and instruct him on a personal basis. He wanted to learn more of God's Word.

One day after a learning session, the chief awkwardly and nervously confessed to the missionary how he, the chief, and several of his men had approached the missionary's house one dark night a few years previous. Their plan and intent was to kill the entire family.

When the missionary asked why they had not carried out their plan, the chief explained that as the band of would-be killers approached the house, they saw it was surrounded by several strange men. These men were dressed in white clothing and brandished swords of fire. From that moment on, the frightened chief had declared the missionary house "off limits" to his cohorts, and commanded that no one in that family was to be harmed.

Perhaps we could call experiences like these "Close Encounters of the Celestial Kind." These few stories are not told to give the false impression that nothing can happen to a Christian because of the security of angels hedging them about. These stories are just examples of God's supernatural power of intervention into humanity when He deems it necessary for His glory and purpose.

In order **not to** give a false impression of assuming that we will always be rescued in time of trouble, we need to be reminded of the millions of wonderful Christians who have suffered in jails (Viz., Joseph; Jeremiah; Paul; John Bunyan; martyrs of the Dark Ages; Christians in Communist and Islamic countries; et al). Christians endured cruel tortures and were put to death without an angel coming to deliver them. It has been estimated that 50-60 million Christians were put to death by state-churches during the European Inquisitions and during The Dark Ages (600-1500 AD. These murders were committed in the name of Christ's religion. Many true Christians suffered horrible torture –

46

(See *Fox's Book of Martyrs; Trail of the Blood; History of the Baptists*; etc.).

How Are Angels Associated With the Church?

In *I Corinthians 11*, the observation by angels are mentioned in connection with the true worship of the church.

> *I Corinthians 11:10: For this cause ought the woman to have <u>power on her head</u> because of the angels.*

It is a matter of **creation**, **authority**, and **order (protocol)**. Paul says that the head of the woman is the man; that the head of the man is Christ, and that the head of Christ is God (I Corinthians 11:3). The woman has her place in the church given to her by the Lord. That place is revealed in I Timothy, Titus, and I Corinthians:

> *I Timothy 2:11-12: Let the women **learn in silence** with all **subjection**. But I suffer **not a woman to teach**, **nor to usurp authority** over the man, but **to be in silence**.*

> *I Timothy 2:13-14: For* (in the creation) ***Adam was first formed**, then Eve. And Adam was not deceived, but the woman being deceived was in the transgression.*

> *I Corinthians 11:13: Judge in yourselves: is it comely that **a woman** pray unto God **uncovered**?*

God has given man first place both in *creation* and *ministry*. These Scriptures are not intending to demean the sexual gender of women but is one of protocol. Neither are the Scriptures saying that women are spiritually inferior to man or that God loves women less than man (or that women

47

love God less than men). Spiritually speaking, women get the job done (spiritually) many times because man is derelict in his duty and service to God. Actually, women bear the spiritual leadership in many homes, because of man's slackness and dereliction to duty (or perhaps the husband is unsaved). The writer is convinced that women have been the spiritual leaders in most of our homes down through the centuries.

Observe that man is to pray and worship with his **head uncovered** (no long hair) because he represents authority. His uncovered head is a token of his order and authority vested in him by God Himself.

When a man's head is covered (with long hair), Paul accounts it a thing against nature:

I Corinthians 11:14: Doth not even nature itself teach you, that, if a man have long hair, it is a shame unto him?

Apparently, long hair on a man is associated with the perversion of his sexual gender and his leadership role. A man with long hair, in the likeness of a woman, is called a shame. Paul goes on to say that if a man wants to be contentious (argue) about it, the churches of God have no such customs as the practice of tolerating or approving long hair on men and short hair on women – (I Corinthians 11:15-16). Nature is a great teacher for the obvious conduct of identifying sexual gender. The writer does not think that a spiritually minded Christian will use his liberty in Christ to argue for the privilege of adding a few more inches of hair length under the guise of, "How long is long? A mature Christian man will agree to a reasonable hair length in order to maintain peace, harmony, and proper order.

Notice that the woman is to have her **head covered** (long hair) as an outward sign and evidence that she is in subjection to God and her husband. The woman's hair shows

48

her modesty and subjection. The Scriptures say that a woman's **long hair** is her covering (veil) and glory (I Corinthians 11:15). This is in contrast to the fashion of women shorning their head; the Bible teaches that she should be covered (long hair). This covering is likened unto long hair or a veil that modest women wore in the East to show their subjection. No doubt, this is the reason that Christian women formerly wore bonnets and still wear hats in church houses today; they reckon that the "head-covering" may include the wearing of a hat or bonnet as well as long hair.

> *I Corinthians 11:7: For a man indeed ought **not to cover his head**, forasmuch as he is the image and glory of God: but the woman is the glory of the man.*

In conclusion and because of the unseen angels, a clear distinction of sexual gender representing male sexual authority, and the woman's "in subjection" position should be established lest these angels who are looking on from above be confused concerning the authority and order (or sexual gender) of man and woman. This would apply especially to the church (I Corinthians 14:34, 35; I Timothy 2:11, 12; Titus 2:5) as well as elsewhere. Remember, angels are not omniscient. All things should be done decently and in order (I Corinthians 14:40). The male/female sexual nomenclature (order; role; system, position) is of God as Scriptures clearly demonstrate by the natural order of hair length for man and woman.

Worship of Angels

Though angels are magnificent, powerful, and very lofty celestial creatures, they are still created beings that are not to be worshipped. Some spiritist type religionists, who are seeking to enhance their ministry, present stories of being entertained by angels in their dreams and visions. Of course, this writer believes the dreams are either concocted religious facades, or demonic manifestations that are common among those in various circles.

> *Colossians 2:18: Let no man beguile you of your reward in a voluntary humility and **worshipping of angels**, intruding into those things which he hath not seen, vainly puffed up by his fleshly mind.*

Can Fallen Angels Be Redeemed?

> *Hebrews 2:16 For verily he took not on him the nature of angels; but he took on him the seed of Abraham.* {took not...: Gr. taketh not hold of angels, but of the seed of Abraham he taketh hold}

> *17. Wherefore in all things it behoved him to be made like unto his brethren, that he might be a merciful and faithful high priest in things pertaining to God, to make reconciliation for the sins of the people. -Php 2:7; Heb 4:15; 5:1-2*

Jesus did not take on a body of angels but of the seed of Abraham (angels do not die). The angels fell and Jesus let them go, without hope or help. Christ never purposed to be Saviour of fallen angels. As their tree fell, it must lie for all eternity. The fallen angels had been in the very presence of God and were totally without excuse for their rebellion. Christ did not assume the nature of angels

Unbiblical Ideas About Angels

'Tis the season of angels! At Christmas time angels are brought to our attention more than any other time of the year. Angel objects are everywhere you look and they come in just about every shape and size imaginable. Manufacturers offer angel ornaments, cards, fine art, books, jewelry, figurines, cologne, undergarments, sleepwear, body wash and makeup. On one website I found a whole host of angel pins that includes a military and patriotic angel that proudly waves the American flag...." (by Marsha West http://www.newswithviews.com/West/marsha59.htm)

PART II

WHO ARE THE SONS OF GOD IN GENESIS?

This section of the angels as the sons of God is largely the writer's opinions and he realizes that his opinions may not be shared by the reader; however, may we agree to disagree in love. The writer absolutely makes no claim of divine guidance but adheres to his limited spiritual discernment.

Among fundamentalist Bible believers, the issue of the identity of "the sons of God" and "the daughters of men" of Genesis chapter six has been one of the most controversial topics. On many subjects of the Bible, there may be various interpretations (or opinions) by Bible students and theologians, but on this subject there appears to be only two prominent interpretations (or opinions) that survive time. Actually, there is only ONE true interpretation of a Bible passage though there may be many applications and opinions.

Some do not consider the controversial text of the sons of God and the daughter of men to be a favorable subject to quibble over; therefore they say, it should not be a viable text for a solid exposition. However, it is in Scriptures and anything in Scriptures is worthy to be searched out. It is a text that can instill a strong biblical base. It will serve to strengthen a Bible student so as not to be blown about with every wind of doctrine.

This subject can also familiarize the student with means of interpretation. Besides, Bible believers are to sharpen the countenance of their brethren by ministering spiritual helps to each other - ("Iron sharpeneth iron" - Proverbs 27:17).

The text of Genesis chapter six itself is not controversial; it is just the interpretations

> *Genesis 6:1-8: And it came to pass, when* **men** *of the earth, and* **daughters** *were born unto them, That* **the sons of God** *saw* **the daughters of men** *that they were fair; and they took them* **wives** *of all which they chose. And the LORD said, My spirit shall not always strive with man, for that he also is* **flesh***: yet his days shall be an hundred and twenty years. There were* **giants** *in the earth in those days; and also after that, when* **the sons of God** *came in unto* **the daughters of men***, and they* **bare children** *to them, the same became* **mighty men** *which were of old,* **men of renown***. And God saw that the wickedness of man was great in the earth, and that every imagination of the thoughts of his heart was only evil continually. And it repented the LORD that he had made man on the earth, and it grieved him at his heart. And the LORD said, I will destroy man whom I have created from the face of the earth; both man, and beast, and the creeping thing, and the fowls of thee air; for it repenteth me that I have made them. But Noah found grace in the eyes of the LORD.*

The writer will only explore three translations (or interpretations; opinions):

Interpretation Number One

Godly men married ungodly women:

This interpretation of Genesis chapter 6 says that "the sons of God" were godly descendants of Seth that married the "daughters of men" of the ungodly line of Cain. This claim is that the offspring of this conjugation of godly men with ungodly women produced men of renown or men with giant intelligence. In other words, the claim is that godly believers were unequally yoked together with ungodly unbelievers and that yoke produced children of a higher intellect and offspring of a greater caliber, which were called "mighty men of renown" (Genesis 6:1-4). This interpretation is favored by most Bible students and theologians (but not fully by the writer).

Some commentators of this interpretation say that the giants mentioned in Genesis 6:4 is a sudden shift to another subject and that the giants have nothing to do with "children born unto the daughters of men." Perhaps so, but If so, it is interesting that the mention of giants is sandwiched between the two parallel verses that were warnings against the then present evil and the coming judgment of God (Genesis 6:3 and Genesis 6:5). Of course, "the men of renown or greater intelligence" of Genesis 6:4 is incongruent (not in harmony with), being encapsulated between the other two verses warning of God's judgment.

Questions concerning Interpretation Number One

Question # 1: An unequal yoke is a common occurrence throughout Bible generations and dispensations! Why would the unequal yoke of believers with unbelievers cause mighty men of renown or men of greater intelligence? It appears that the opposite would be true of an unequal yoke with evil unbelievers!

54

Question # 2: Why would the mere unequal yoke between a believer and an unbeliever cause a worldwide flood and destruction of all mankind (except Noah's family)? Again, unequal yokes are prevalent in every generation.

Question # 3: Why were believers in the New Testament admonished to stay with the unbelieving spouse if the "unequal yoke" was such a monstrous sin that demanded capital judgment of the entire world (I Corinthians 7:10-16).

Question # 4: If the "sons of God" were so godly, why didn't they get on the boat with Noah? In the same context of this era of alleged "godly men," Genesis 6:5 says, "And God saw that the wickedness of man was great in the earth, and that every imagination of the thoughts of man only evil continually." Actually, the godly people were on the boat, just eight of them. Neither is there any record of these "so-called" godly men ever helping Noah build the Ark (that was a **long time** in building) Of course, we are not told, but unbelievers may have been employed by Noah in building the ark).

Question # 5: Where is there a *godly line* of people in Scriptures? Even the human bloodline of Messiah Jesus was tainted. **Judah** was an adulterer and **Tamar** was an adulteress. **Pharez** was an illegitimate child (a bastard child); Later, **Rahab** had been a harlot; **Bathsheba** was an adulteress; **David** committed adultery, lied, and murdered Uriah, Bathsheba's husband. **Solomon** loved many strange women and his wives turned away his heart when he was old (I Kings 11:1-9). Christ's human genealogy also runs through wicked kings of Israel.

If the Interpretation of godly men marrying evil women is the absolute correct one, the Scriptures would plainly say, "The godly lineage of the sons of Seth married into the ungodly lineage or wicked lineage of the daughters of Cain?"

Question # 6: If the "sons of God" of Genesis 6:2 are of the godly line of Seth, why did the Scriptures not say so? If the sons of God were of the godly line of Seth, who were these other sons of God that were present when the foundation of the earth was laid, before Adam and Eve were created? (Job 38:4-7)

Question # 7: If the "daughters of men" of Genesis 6:2 are of the ungodly line of Cain, why did the Scriptures not say so?

Question # 8: If the prophetical seed of "the woman" in Genesis 3:15 is a literal prophecy of *Jesus Christ* being born into human lineage, why should it be thought impossible that the "seed of the serpent" (Antichrist; Satan incarnate; Demonic manifestation) could literally enter somehow into the human DNA lineage? If the seed of the woman is literal in Genesis 3:15, so is the seed of the serpent literal in this same verse!

Example: Bible students readily accept the part of Genesis 3:15 as being a literal prophetic fulfillment concerning the prophecy of Christ via the seed of woman, but then relegate the part of the same verse prophesying the seed of the serpent as merely a figurative expression. Please explain why one is literal and the other is only figurative.

Next, we consider questions concerning the literal interpretation Number Two of the sons of God as fallen angels cohabiting with the daughter of men:

Interpretation Number Two

Fallen angels cohabited with earth women:

Interpretation number two says that "the sons of God" were fallen angels that left their first estate and literally cohabited with the "daughters of men" (earth women). They claim that this bizarre and ungodly perversion produced children that became huge giants. They believe that it was Satan's plan to interject Antichrist into the human lineage through an ungodly form of sexual conjugation that would affect or alter the human genome and defeat God's purpose with mankind upon earth.

Question # 1: If the conjugation of fallen angels with daughters of men caused giants of great physical stature, how can we explain the many physical giants of all ages and even of **today**? We have basketball players over seven feet tall and there have been other giants in the modern world over eight feet tall (Of course, we know that the pituitary endocrine gland secretes hormones that greatly affect body growth and metabolism).

So what caused the physical giants **after** the flood (called, Zuzims, Anakims, Rephaims, and Zamzummims)? Was this a repeat of the alleged angels of Genesis chapter six of cohabiting with earth women? Goliath, of whom David slew **after** the flood, was a giant who had four brethren. Are giants of today the result of angels cohabiting with daughters of men or are they just a continuation of past genetic contamination of a lessened effect?(Note: Even the giants of today are smaller than OT giants - I Samuel 17:4.)

Question # 2: If angels (alleged fathers of giants) appear upon earth the size of mortal men, why would their offspring be giants?(Again, some think that such a conjugation of evil angels would alter the genetic anatomical makeup.)

Question # 3: Why were all of the giant-offspring of the sons of God and the daughters of men always **men**? There is no mention of giant-women (though there might have been).

Question # 4: If evil "daughters of men" of Genesis 6:2 cohabited with fallen angels, why not expressly say so? (Perhaps it was explicitly stated.)

Question # 5: If the "sons of God" of Genesis 6:2 are fallen angels, why was it not expressly stated?

Question # 6: Other than the controversial passage of Genesis chapter six, it does not appear that the *fallen* angels have the authority to transform themselves as men (we know that the *good* angels [unfallen angels] are able to appear as ordinary men).If "fallen angels" cannot transform themselves as men, how could the alleged sons of God cohabit with the daughters of men? There is no biblical text of" fallen" angels appearing in the form of a man.

Question # 7: Why would the angels (all male gender) have male reproductive components if they never die and do not have to reproduce themselves? (Of course, supporters of theory #2 claim that fallen angels were able to conjugate with women upon earth.)

Question # 8: Why would God allow such an unnatural and bizarre yoke of fallen angels and earth women?(With this somewhat bold and fuzzy question, there is absolutely no intent to intrude upon God's sovereignty nor is there any attempt to elevate man to God's supreme level of understanding.)

Question # 9: Why aren't the alleged fallen sons of God addressed in the similitude of the "devil's angels" as we find in Matthew 25:41?

Which side of the controversy does the writer endorse?

This writer will play the role of "the devil's advocate" by critiquing both sides of the controversy as the reader may have already observed (everybody hates the middle-man). There is a lot to be said, both pro and con, of both prominent interpretations (or opinions). The writer has posed a few hard questions for either of the two commonly accepted positions on the issue. The writer does not fully endorse either of these two accepted interpretations and prefers a third interpretation (or opinion) which follows.

Interpretation Number Three

The seed of the serpent is (or, "will be") a literal manifestation of Antichrist through Demonic possession:

In this writer's opinion, demonic possession is the favored interpretation of the identity of the sons of God. It appears that demons are fallen angels (sons of God of which a certain segment of them became dispossessed of their bodies) These evil fallen sons of God of dispossessed bodies (demons) had left their first estate (Jude 6) and indwelt and possessed evil men that afterwards cohabited with the daughters of men (there were no angel daughters). In this way, it could be said that fallen angels (sons of God) could possess bodies of men and cohabit with the daughters of men (not necessarily marry). Again, this scenario is that of fallen angels of dispossessed bodies yearning to possess literal human male bodies (some demons requested of Christ to be cast into swine). This interpretation (or the writer's opinion) could fit the literal interpretation of the seed of the serpent as well as that of the seed of the woman of Genesis 3:15. Again, if the prophecy of the seed of the woman of Genesis 3:15 is literal, so then is the prophecy of the seed of the serpent also literal.

C. I. Scofield's Bible notes: Scofield, favors most of the writer's Christian friends of an ungodly line of Cain's descendants (called daughters of men) marrying into a godly line of Seth's descendants (called sons of God).

The writer does not see any justification for breaking fellowship over the different interpretations (or opinions) of the text of Genesis chapter 6.

Since many Bible students are familiar with **C. I. Scofield's** Bible notes, Mr. Scofield's comments will serve to support the position of **Interpretation Number One,** that of the "ungodly line of Cain marrying into the godly line of Seth." C. I. Scofield was an excellent theologian and Bible scholar in this writer's opinion, but he was fallible and "may have" erred in his interpretation (not necessarily incorrect) of the sons of God and the daughters of men. The writer believes that Scofield was a man of unquestionable integrity and even recommends his Scofield Reference Bible (KJV with Scofield notes), with precautions of course (because of a few faulty notes and comments of a debatable nature).

(**NOTE:** The writer acknowledges that Bible commentators have faults just as do ALL men. However, when an exegetical examination is expressed in terms of conclusive exposition without any fanfare or hint as being the commentator's opinion, this writer objects. Many times, perhaps the main problem lies in "commentators copying other commentators" and so on, without greater examination. There are times that writers are under pressures of limited time and substance to complete their publications. No doubt, we all are guilty of this to some degree.)

Scofield says on page 13 of the Scofield Reference Bible that angels are spoken of in a sexless way, they do not marry (Matthew 22:30), and no 'female' angels are mentioned in Scripture." (Note: all Scofield Bibles have the same page numbers.)

COMMENT: This statement is a contradiction of terms in itself. Scofield's statement that "no female angels are mentioned" implies that the angels then mentioned are all male angels. He is undoubtedly correct in assuming that all angels are male, but this also contradicts his statement that they are sexless (Unless he meant that they do not sexually reproduce themselves). Saying that there are no female angels is the same as saying that angels are all males. Numerous times in Scriptures, masculine pronouns are used in reference to angels (**he**) – Matthew 28:2-4; 2 Samuel 24:16; I Chronicles 21:15; Acts 12:7; Revelation 22:8, 9). Adding to this, the angels who are named have masculine names, Michael; Gabriel; Lucifer. Of course, even in the OT and down through the centuries, men and women use the same names of similar and identical spellings.

Dale and Dell, Frances and Francis are modern examples.

Scofield correctly quotes Matthew 22:30 where it is said that angels do not marry in Heaven.

COMMENT: But this does not absolutely rule out a perverted relationship upon earth of angels of dispossessed bodies (sons of God; demons) and daughters of men; neither do humans marry or re-marry in Heaven. However bizarre and ungodly it may appear (even as the unthinkable and ungodly "bestiality" of Leviticus 18:23), Jesus did not say that fallen angels (sons of God) cannot indirectly affect the DNA of mankind upon earth, but He does say, **"in Heaven they do not marry"** (or cohabit).

Perhaps it was the goal of Satan in the beginning to somehow taint the human blood line and affect the human genome in order to defeat God's eternal Plan of the Ages. Nothing is too bizarre or horrible for Satan and his demons. Supernatural acts of demonic activity will greatly increase at the close of the age just as in the days of Noah (Matthew 24:37). There are many horrible acts of mutilation and murder committed by people under the influence of drugs and demonic possession. There is one horrible modern case where a drug-crazed person cooked a live baby in a micro wave oven, perhaps assuming or thinking it was a chicken or a turkey (or did not even care).

Scofield goes on to say that Genesis 6:2 marks the breaking down between the godly line of Seth and the ungodly line of Cain.

COMMENT: **If** there were two such lines, it is for certain that they would break down. There is no argument here. This statement may not challenge either interpretation.

(Note: This "alleged" godly line did not exist when Noah's Flood came upon the earth. If the godly line had been in existence, they would have been on the ark with Noah.)

Dr. John D. Morris of the *Institute for Creation Research* makes some interesting comments concerning the giants in the days of Noah.

> *Genesis 6:4: There were **giants** in the earth in those days; and also after that, when **the sons of God** came in unto **the daughters of men**, and they bare children to them.*

Dr. Morris says, "Few passages in all of Scripture have yielded so many interpretations as Genesis 6:1-5. Who were the "sons of God"? Who were the "daughters of men"? Why would their union produce giants and be associated with great wickedness?

Some have proposed that the "sons of God" were the descendants of Adam's son Seth, and the "daughters of men" were from the line of rebellious Cain. An interesting thought, but in Noah's day there were essentially no righteous people, from any line.

Others have rightly noted that the term "sons of God" in the Old Testament refers only to angels (or Adam), thus these must be the fallen angels. Satan had launched an aggressive campaign against Adam and his descendants in an attempt to so pollute mankind that the promised

Redeemer, the "seed of the woman" (Genesis 3:15) could not come.

"But angels in Scripture are spiritual beings having no permanent body, and in heaven, at least, they do not "marry" (Matthew 22:30). And just what would this half angel/half man be? Would it be a giant, and more importantly, would it have an eternal spirit?

"Let me suggest another alternative from our modern-day understanding of genomics, one which Bible scholars of yesteryear could not have suggested.

"I suspect that if today's geneticist and molecular biologist can accomplish such technical wonders as gene splicing and cloning, that the much greater intelligence of Satan could potentially have done it too. The inner workings of the DNA molecule would not have been hidden from the prying eyes of Satan and his henchmen. If today animal genes can be inserted into human DNA, could not it have been accomplished by malevolent spiritual beings bent on destruction of the "image of God"?

"Obviously we cannot speak with certainty; for the Bible gives little detail. At the very least, Satan's demons could have selected and indwelt certain men and women, and performed selective breeding experiments to produce over the generations a race of giants. (He could have done the same with animals too, and maybe that's where some of the unthinkable features we see in the fossil record come from. This could represent Satan's rage in trying to fully destroy any vestige of God's once very good creation.) Could he not have inserted genes and fabricated clones, mocking and ruining God's majestic handiwork? Perhaps this is why God had to send the Flood, eradicating a civilization beyond repair and starting anew with Noah, preserving the true seed of Adam.

"One more thought. Christ compared the days of Noah to the days prior to His return. Are the actions which produce "giants," whatever they were, considered in this comparison? Certainly at no prior time of history have humans been able to "play God" with the genome as they do now. The rush to embrace the ghoulish possibilities of cloning and embryonic stem cell manipulation may be reminiscent of that long ago time. God's utter condemnation of that effort may help us evaluate modern experiments" - (*Institute for Creation Research* © 2002, February 2002, P.O. Box 2667, El Cajon, CA 92021).

This writer (dh) has observed that today there are serious studies and actual experiments of attempts to insert DNA of various animals genes into the human genome in an effort to make a super-soldier (Viz., one of strength; endurance; speed; sight; instincts; et al).

Digressing Into the Heretical Doctrines of William Marrion Branham

The reader may prefer to refrain from reading about Branham's and Arnold Murray's heresies but provides the information for those that may be interested.

In William Marrion Branham's book, *An Exposition of the Seven Church Ages*, Charismatic William Branham makes some outlandish claims concerning Adam's son, Cain. Among many other heretical teachings, Branham claims that Cain is the hybrid son of the sexual conjugation between the serpent and Eve. Now Branham does not mean a fallen angel (as a demon or the devil) but a literal serpent as in a sexual relationship of bestiality between a woman (Eve) and a snake. He claims that this sexual conjugation of a human (Eve) and an animal (snake; serpent) produced Adam's son, Cain. Branham main basis for his belief of the serpent being Cain's daddy is the New Testament verse of I

John 3:12 – *"Not as Cain, who was of that* wicked *one* (the serpent) *and slew his brother."* Branham and his protege, Arnold Murray *(*of the *Shepherds Chapel* TV airing*), claim that* a literal serpent or snake is meant here. Again, Branham and Murray propose that Eve and a literal serpent (snake) had sexual conjugation (bestiality) and produced a son called Cain. It is strange how easily these two heretics overlook Genesis 4:1 where the Scriptures clearly tell us that Adam knew (sexual) his wife; and she conceived, and bare Cain. I presume that means that Adam was the father of Cain, not the serpent or snake. There is a vast and insurmountable gulf between a woman conjugating with a demon possessed man (or fallen angel of sorts) and that of a woman conjugating with a snake and bearing a son.

To show the proverbial "Monkey see, monkey do" effect of one heretic upon another, Branham's protégé, Arnold Murray (now deceased) of Gravette, Arkansas, infers that Cain, as a Kenite survived the flood by being a passenger in Noah's Ark - (see Arnold Murray's cassette tape, *The Mark of the Beast*).

The Bible plainly declares that there were only eight (8) people on the ark

> *Genesis 7:7, 13, 23: And Noah went in, and his sons, and his wife, and his sons wives with him, into the ark, because of the waters of the flood. In the selfsame day entered **Noah**, and **Shem**, and **Ham**, and **Japheth**, the sons of Noah, and **Noah's wife**, and **the three wives of his sons** with them, into the ark: And every living substance was destroyed which was upon the face of the ground, both man, and cattle, and the creeping things, and the fowl of the heaven; and they were destroyed from the earth: and Noah only remained alive and they that were with him in the ark.*

To sum up Branham's ludicrous *exegesis* (interpretation of a word or passage), he says that Cain persevered through time (even on Noah's ark) as a Kenite and was the serpent that bruised Jesus' heel.

There is much rhetoric concerning the word, "Cain," by Branham simply because Cain is derived from the same root word as, Cainan, Kenite, Kenan, and Canaan, which the writer will briefly reply to.

Branham's theory (and Murray's) is supposed to mean that Cain went through the flood with Noah's family and was later sustained after the flood as a Kenite. And this whole theory is propped up on two main observations:

✓ The two words "Cain" and "Kenite" shares the same root word

✓ 2.) I John 3:12 says, "Cain was of that wicked one" which the heretics twist to mean that Cain was the son of a literal serpent (snake).

1) The writer has searched out the root meaning of "Kenite" and found no basis to support the wacky theory that Cain survived the flood in the person of a Kenite along with Noah's family. Cain did not survive the flood and later manifest himself as a Kenite, as Branham and Murray ignorantly and falsely suggest; however, the wicked spirit of Cain's false religion did re-propagate itself through his father, the devil (John 8:44**)**, who is also called a serpent in other biblical passages (Revelation 20:2).

(The Midianites, or Kenites, descended from Abraham through his second wife Keturah - Genesis 25:2. They can be traced through Moses' father-in-law, Jethro, who was a Midianite - Exodus 18:1; Judges 4:11; and through Caleb, the son of Hur, see I Chronicles 2:50-55. Kenites are found in the following references, Judges 1:16;

4:11, 17; 5:25; I Samuel 15:6; 10; 30:29; I Chronicles 2:55; Genesis 15:19; Numbers 24:21-22.)

2) The Kenites were among one of the 10 tribes of Canaan in the time of Abraham [Genesis 15:19]. Kenites, [Hebrew "ha-qeni," smith, pertaining to coppersmiths] were metal smiths who traveled throughout the mineral-bearing region in the Wadi Arabah. The Kenites descended from the Midianites. The Midianites were the descendants of Abraham by his second wife Keturah [Genesis 25:1-2, 4; I Chronicles 1:32-33]. They early settled down along the S.W. shore of the Dead Sea, S.E. of Hebron [Judges 1:16; 4:11]. They were found in the Wadi Arabah [Numbers 24:20-22], in Naphtali [Judges 4:11] and in the Davidic-Solomonic era are mentioned in southern Judah [I Samuel 15:6; 27:10].Heber [Judges 4:11; 5:24] was a Kenite and the ascetic Rechabites [I Chronicles 2:55] were also of Kenite extraction.)

The Sons of God in the OT versus the Sons of God in the NT

There appears to be a differentiation between the sons of God in the Old Testament from the sons of God in the New Testament. Both OT and NT believers are referred to as "saints." The sons of God in the OT were creatures of direct creation (angels; Adam; even Eve) and the sons of God in the NT are creatures of re-creation (born again) of the eternal indwelling of the Holy Spirit (John 14:16; 17:21, 22; 2 Corinthians 5:17; John 3-3-7).

Angels were called sons of God because they had no parents and were created entities (Job 1:6; 2:1; 6:2; 38:7). Of course, this is the reason that Adam was called the son of God. In the OT, the title "sons of God" is used five times (Genesis 6:2; 6:4; Job 1:6; 2:1; 38:7). Each time, it appears to be in reference to angels (fallen and unfallen). While we may disagree on the issue of what the sons of God might mean in Genesis chapter 6, we cannot argue the point in the book of Job for the terminology of "the sons of God" clearly refers to the angels who were present at Creation (before man was created upon earth on the sixth day). Those who support the Scofield position say that 'sons of God' refer to believers in the OT as well as the NT (and loosely speaking, there is a general sense in which this may be a valid point). However, there does appear to be a definite difference between the two. We are told in Job 1:6 that Satan (not unfallen Lucifer) appeared among the sons of God who had come to present themselves before the LORD. Apparently, this is a time after Lucifer's rebellion, since he is addressed as Satan. If the sons of God in *Genesis 6* were mere men of the godly line of Seth, how could they present themselves before the Lord in Heaven and Satan also among them? How can two walk together except they be agreed? Of course, this occasion preceded Christ's First Coming to earth. Could a "godly" line of Seth appear before God in Heaven (in body or spirit) with Satan before Christ had even paid the price for the redemption of man? The writer thinks not! And when Satan appeared before God, those present with him would likely be fallen angels or sons of God, not true followers of God.

Looking now at Job 38:4-10 (paraphrasing), The LORD says, "Job, where were you (though a great man on earth) or any other man, when I laid the foundation of the earth? When I laid the measures thereof; When the "morning stars" sang together; When "the sons of God" shouted for joy; When I made the cloud a garment and thick darkness a swaddling band for it; And set bars and doors...?" When God laid the foundation of the earth, man was not yet created; consequently, neither Job nor any other human sons of God existed at this time (Man himself was created on the sixth day of the creation week after the laying of earth's foundation). So whoever the "sons of God" were, they could not have been men of renown or more intelligent human beings from earth. That only leaves celestial forms of life, such as angels. Again, it is quite obvious that man did not precede the beginning of creation, a time before man even existed. The angels (*sons of God*) shouted for joy (note the plural number of "sons of God," not a lone man, as Adam). However, Adam could be called a "son of God" because he was "created" by God, not born of woman and man. Why would the sons of God here (Job 38) means something different from the sons of God of Genesis chapter 6?

In the OT, the title "sons of God" obviously appears to pertain to celestial life (angels) and is opposed to terrestrial natural life. Perhaps it could be said, the **angels** in the Old Testament were referred to as sons of God because they were creatures of "direct" Creation (as Adam is called "son of God" in Luke 3:38). New Testament believers are referred to as sons of God because they are "re-created" and "indwelt" of the spiritual birth by the Holy Spirit (John 3:3, 5, 7; 2 Corinthians 5:17; I Corinthians 12:13; I Peter 1:23).

> *2 Corinthians 5:17: Therefore if any man be in Christ, he is **a new creature**: old things are passed away; behold, all things are become new.*

> *John 1:12-13: But as many as received Him, to them gave He power to become **the sons of God**, even to them that believe on His name: Which were born, not of blood, nor of the will of the flesh, nor of the will of man, but of God.*

> *John 3:3, 7-8: Jesus answered and said unto him, Verily, verily, I say unto thee, Except a man be **born again**, he cannot see the kingdom of God. Marvel not that I said unto thee, Ye must be born again. The wind bloweth where it listeth, and thou hearest the*

*sound thereof, but canst not tell whence it cometh, and whither it goeth: so is every one that is **born of the Spirit**.*

(Jesus brought grace and truth to the NT dispensation of grace and told Nicodemus, who was under law, that he must be "born again;" however, OT saints were not indwelt permanently by the Holy Spirit before Pentecost, as are NT saints.)

*I John 3:1-2: Behold, what manner of love the Father hath bestowed upon us, that we should be called **the sons of God**: therefore the world knoweth us not, because it knew Him not. Beloved, now are we **the sons of God**, and it doth not yet appear what we shall be: but we know that, when he shall appear, we shall be like him; for we shall see Him as He is.*

*Romans 8:9: But ye are not in the flesh, but in the Spirit, if so be that the **Spirit of God dwell in you**. Now if any man have not the Spirit of Christ, he is none of his.*

See Galatians 4:6; Romans 8:14-16.

Nicodemus and the New Birth

Jesus instructed Nicodemus, a Jewish member of the 70-member ruling body of the Jewish Sanhedrin, about salvation (some think 71 members). Nicodemus was a master of Jewish Law, and Jesus lovingly chided him for not knowing that he must be born-again (John 3:1-10; 2 Corinthians 5:17).

At the time of Nicodemus, Jesus had not yet died and arisen for the justification of all believers and NT believers had not yet received the "indwelling" of the Holy Spirit (the time of Pentecost had not yet come); consequently, saints could not qualify as new creations (or 'sons of God'). The NT Jews were told to wait for the coming of the Holy Spirit at the time of Pentecost. Before Pentecost and under Mosaic law, saints were indwelt piece-meal for a time only (Psalms 51:11). The Holy Spirit was poured out in His fullness at Pentecost (Acts 2).

Since the supreme sacrifice of Jesus Christ for sin had not yet been paid for before Calvary, there was a sense in which believers were saved on credit. The OT sacrifices merely held off the wrath of God from year to year until the perfect sacrifice by Christ could pay the full and final price for sin. Of course, the debt now having been paid in full and the fulfilling of the promise of the coming of the indwelling Holy Spirit at Pentecost, the NT saints (both Jew and Gentile) could well be called "sons of God."

Jesus Called "The Son of God"

Jesus is the **ONLY BEGOTTEN** Son of God. The Son of God in the sense of "Creation" does not apply to Jesus as it does to Adam (Luke 3:38). Adam was called the son of God because he was created and not born of woman. Jesus has always existed and there is none like Him anywhere. Jesus is unique in that He is **in** the bosom of the Father (John 1:18). Jesus is Creator and the Creator does not Create Himself.

> *Hebrews 1:5: For unto which of the angels said He at any time, Thou art My Son, this day have I begotten Thee? And again, I will be to him a Father, and he shall be to me a Son?*

Hebrews 1:5 is a quotation from Psalms 2:7 that points to the day of **Jesus' resurrection** when He was begotten again from the dead.

71

Acts 13:33: God hath fulfilled the same unto us their children, in that he hath raised up Jesus again; as it is also written in the second psalm, Thou art My Son, this day have I begotten Thee.

Colossians 1:18: And he is the head of the body, the church: who is the beginning, the firstborn from the dead; that in all things he might have the preeminence.

-Jesus has neither beginning of days, nor end of life (Hebrews 7:3).

Jesus as He that shall come forth *"to be ruler in Israel; whose goings forth have been from of old, from everlasting"* (Micah 5:2).

As John 1:18 declares, *"...the only Begotten Son, which is in the bosom of the Father..."*

Christ is not the *only* Son of God but He is *The Only Begotten Son of God* just as it is in the Greek Textus Receptus of the KJV.

Sons of God and a Son of God

In the OT, both a "son of God" (not The Son of God, Jesus) and the "sons of God" denote beings brought into existence by a direct **creative act of God**. Such was **Adam who was Created** (Luke 3:38). This would also include the created angels.

The writer has scanned the OT and has observed that ALL other sons than the "sons of God" of Genesis chapter six and those of the book of Job, were naturally **born** into existence, not directly created. Those that were not directly created were called "sons of man" or "sons of men" (Proverbs 8:4; Ecclesiastes 1:13; 2:3; 3:10, 18; 9:3, 12;

Psalms 57:4; 58:1; 145:12; Joel 1:12). Consequently, they were always called "sons of....Adam; Noah; Japheth; Ham; Shem; Gomer; Cush; Jacob; Ishmael Esau; Leah; Belial; Israel;" etc.) Other than Adam and the angels, no man or men are called by the specific terms "the son of God," or "the sons of God" in the OT.

> *Luke 3:38: Which was the **son of Enos**, which was the **son of Seth**, which was the **son of Adam**, which was **the son of God.***

Again, Adam was **not** naturally birthed. He did not have human parents; thus it could be said that he was "a son of God" by creation, not by birth. Adam's natural descendants were not of the direct creation of God but were born in Adam's likeness (Genesis 5:3). Consequently, all men born of Adam and his descendants by natural generation in the OT, are "the sons of men" (or daughters of men). It is only by the new creation (re-creation) that we can become the sons of God in the NT sense. It is from "natural generation" (natural birth) to "washing of regeneration" (supernatural birth). See Titus 3:5.

> *2 Corinthians 5:17: If any man be in Christ, he is a **new creature** (creation)...*

If the "sons of God" are angels in Genesis 6:2-4 and in the book of Job, they could NOT be the sons of Seth as some claim, because the sons of Seth were only men and could only be called "sons of men," and not, "sons of God." Some refute this claim by stating that there are two references to sons and daughters of God in the OT (Isaiah 43:6; Hosea 1:10); however, it is not the specific terminology of the "sons of God."

Ezekiel of the OT is referred to as "son of man" 90 times (never as "son of God). Even Daniel of the OT is referred to as "son of man" and not "son of God" (Daniel 8:17).

*Isaiah 43:6: I will say to the north, Give up; and to the south, Keep not Back: bring **my sons** from far, and **my daughters** from the ends of the earth.*

*Hosea 1:10: Yet the number of the children of Israel shall be as the sand of the sea, which cannot be measured nor numbered; and it shall come to pass, that in the place where it was said unto them, Ye are not my people, there **it shall be said unto them**, Ye are the **sons of the living God.***

This is prophetically speaking of **Israel's future restoration** in the millennium. The Lord is speaking strictly to Israelites here. The Israelite sons and daughters in Isaiah 43 are not called "godly." Later in the chapter, God chides them because of their wickedness.

In Exodus 4:22:

*And thou shalt say unto Pharaoh, Thus saith the Lord, Israel is **my son**, even my firstborn.*

This is the strongest and only opposition against the claim that angels were the sons of God. These alluded to in these verses are not specifically called by the terminology "sons of God."

Going After "Strange Flesh" Associated With Fallen Angels

There are two particular passages in the New Testament that advocates of Interpretation Number 2 associate in a literal sense.

Reason Number One:

*2 Peter 2:4-7: For if God spared not the **angels that sinned**, but cast them down to*

*Hell, and delivered them into chains of darkness, to be reserved unto judgment; And spared not the old world, but saved Noah the eight person, a preacher of righteousness, bringing in **the flood upon the world** of the ungodly; And turning the cities of **Sodom and Gomorrha** into ashes condemned them with an overthrow, making them an ensample unto those that **after should live ungodly**. And delivered just **Lot, vexed with the filthy conversation** of the wicked.*

The advocates of Interpretation #2 propose that this sin of women and angels, which occurred before the flood, also occurred again even after the flood and produced giant men or angel-men hybrids. They also point to the judgment of God against Sodom and Gomorrha to be directly associated with Noah's Flood (2 Peter 2:4-7). The fallen angels were going after strange flesh even as Lot was vexed with the filthy environment of sodomites. Of course, advocates of an ungodly line marrying a godly line can rightfully question why the earth was only flooded once and not afterwards. The advocates favoring Scofield's "ungodly line marrying a godly line" suppose that the earth should suffer another universal "flood" if angels were again literally cohabiting with earth women as alleged before the flood. Of course, the earth is to be destroyed again but the next time by "fire" (2 Peter 3:6, 10).

Reason Number Two:

*Jude 1:6-7: And **the angels** which kept not their first estate, but **left their own habitation**, He hath reserved in everlasting chains under darkness unto the judgment of the great day. Even **as Sodom and Gomorrha**, and the cities about them in like manner, giving themselves over to fornication, and going **after strange flesh**,*

*are set forth for an example, suffering the
vengeance of eternal fire*

The term "strange flesh' can be expressed in several
ways: Viz., sodomy (homosexuality and lesbianism;
perverted sexual acts; bestiality (sex with animals - Leviticus
18:23); angels of God cohabiting with daughters of men;
fallen angels dispossessed of bodies cohabiting with
daughters of men; et al.

The advocates of angels cohabiting with daughters of
women may ask, "If this was not a bizarre sin between angels
and mankind, why are some fallen angels free and some
chained in darkness?" They also ask, "If all the fallen angels
were equally guilty in following Lucifer in the rebellion,
why aren't all of the fallen angels chained or why aren't all
of the fallen angels free?" Obviously, all of the angels were
not involved in sexually contaminating the bloodline of the
human race just as all angels were not guilty in the angel's
rebellion in Heaven. There is clearly a distinction even
between certain rebellious angels. Some angels roam about
the earth, some angels are cast down to Hell, and some
angels are dispossessed of bodies and relegated to demons
(wicked angels dispossessed of bodies).

It is also said of the fallen angels that they "left their
own habitation," and was not at that time "cast out of
Heaven" as it is later said "cast down to Hell" (2 Peter 2:4).
It does not say that the fallen angels left Heaven, but that the
fallen angels left their "own habitation." (Does "habitation"
mean a location, as in Heaven and earth or does it mean aa
life-style as that of fallen angels (in demon form) cohabiting
with daughters of men?)It appears that the fallen angels may
have chosen an earthly habitat with daughters of men (by
whatever means) over the heavenly habitat. In Revelation
12:9, we are told that Satan and his angels were cast out into
the earth. Again, it is apparent that some fallen angels are
reserved in everlasting chains (Jude 6-7) and some are cast

out into the earth (Revelation 12:9). Some of the fallen angels were cast down into Hell but then again, some of them were dispossessed of bodies and relegated to a demon status which caused them to desire to inhabit a body of whatever sorts (even swine).

(Keep in mind and remember that Section II of this paper is much speculation by the writer and the writer's opinions are not to be charged to God; nor does this writer make any claim of divine guidance).

In the context of Jude 6 and 7, it is obvious that the terms, "angels, Sodom and Gomorrha, fornication, and going after strange flesh" are closely associated. In Sodom and Gomorrha, men lusted after men, a form of a physical, sexual relationship that was bizarre, unnatural (against nature), grotesque, and was forbidden in Scriptures many times (Leviticus 18:22: Romans 1:26, 27). It appears that some of the fallen angels cast out into the earth sought to cohabit with mortals (by some means) in such an unnatural way as to stagger imaginations.

(NOTE: Some have conjectured that Psalm 82:1-7 is alluding to angels. The writer does not think so. It appears that these gods are magistrates, rulers, princes, kings, etc.- John 10:34; Genesis 3:5.)

Why or How an Unnatural Relationship of Fallen Angels and Daughters of Men?

For the **Why**, advocates of "angels cohabiting with women" use *Genesis 6:12* to answer:

> *Genesis 6:12: And God looked upon the earth, and, behold, it was corrupt; for all flesh had corrupted his way upon the earth.*

These advocates say, "In his rebellion, Satan has desired from the very beginning of Creation to defeat God's plan of the ages. Satan even accused God of blessing the patriarch Job with material blessings in order to retain Job's service to God; Satan even dared God to remove His protecting hedge from Job to disprove Job's faithfulness."

It is the book of Job that clearly expresses the "sons of God" as angels who were present when God laid the foundation of the earth. (See Job 38:6-7)

For the **How**, advocates of "angels cohabiting with women" also use *Genesis 3:15*:

> *Genesis 3:15: And I will put enmity between thee and the woman, and **between thy seed and her seed**; it shall bruise thy head, and thou shalt bruise his heel.*

Satan sought to corrupt the blood line of Jesus.

Here again, we have a fallen angelic creatures involved.

Interpretation:

- The woman: Eve; Israel; Mary (Revelation 12:1-6; Genesis 37:9); of course, Jesus was born of the seed of a woman, Mary. A woman has eggs or ova; the man has sperm or seed. Modern science calls both the egg and sperm, gametes. A fertilized egg is called a zygote. Christ's birth was miraculous of the Holy Spirit.

- Her seed: The promised Messiah; Christ (Revelation 12:1-6)

- Thy seed: Primarily Satan's cohort, the Antichrist (Revelation 13:4-8; 2 Thessalonians 2:3-9), but also his lap-dog zombies (Genesis 4:8; Matthew 26:14-16; 27:3; Luke 22:3; John 13:27; 17:12).

- <u>Bruise His heel</u>: A temporary wound to Christ (Psalms 22; Isaiah 53:5-6; Romans 5:8; Hebrews 2:9; 9:26)

- <u>Bruise thy head</u>: A permanent wound to Satan (Revelation 19:20; 20:10)

Satan bruised the heel of Jesus at Calvary's cross (only by God's permission) and Jesus also bruised Satan at Calvary's cross and shall bruise his head permanently at a future time when God casts Satan into the lake of fire with the beast and the false prophet (Revelation 20:10).

Satan's number one henchman, the Antichrist, is called "that man of sin, the son of perdition" (2 Thessalonians 2:3).

<u>Add to the list of the enemies of God</u>: Pharaoh, Antiochus Epiphanes, Haman, Herod, Hitler, and Satan's religious ministers (2 Corinthians 11:13-15).

It is well established by Bible scholars and students alike that Genesis 3:15 is prophetic of the virgin birth of Jesus Christ, the promised Messiah (God's Darling Son):

*Genesis 3:15: And I will put enmity between thee and the woman, and between **thy seed** and **her seed**; it shall bruise thy head, and thou shalt bruise his heel.*

In this Scripture, we have two" literal" future prophecies concerning, thy seed (Satan's) and her seed (Mary's). (Note: Israel is also pictured as a woman – Revelation 12: 1, 2) Genesis 3:15 is the first prophecy in the OT of Christ concerning Jesus' virgin birth of woman. Of course, the "seed of the woman" (Christ) is not merely a figurative statement, but a literal prophecy with a literal fulfillment. Again, and again, if the **seed of the woman** is literal prophecy, then the **seed of the serpent is also** literal prophecy ("...the great dragon, that old serpent, called the

Devil, and Satan, which deceiveth the whole world..." – Revelation 12:9).

It is obvious that Satan will somehow enter into the human lineage by his seed that is defined as "the seed of the serpent. "It also appears logical that the ultimate, evil manifestation of the serpent's seed will be realized through the Antichrist personage of Revelation 13:1-8 (See 2 Thessalonians 2:3, 4, 8-9; I John 2:18; 4:3; 2 John 7; Daniel 2:43). This scenario appears to have been prefigured by Judas Iscariot who is the only other person in the Bible referred to as "diabolos" (devil). It is also said only of both the devil and Judas that they went to "their own place," or to perdition (Hell). God allowed Satan to enter into Judas (Luke 22:3) and betray Jesus which led to the fulfillment of the prophecy of "bruising Christ's heel" at the cross of Calvary. Christ must die for sinners! The writer does not rule out the possibility that perhaps Satan himself will totally possess an ungodly man who will conjugate with a harlot (certainly not a virgin) and produce the Antichrist personage (Revelation 13; 2 Thessalonians 2). If Satan entered into Judas (the thief and betrayer of Christ), he certainly could enter into humanity through a totally demon-possessed man's seed (perhaps affecting the genome). Remember too, we are not told that Satan was of a dispossessed body as a demon when he entered into Judas. Again, if the seed of the woman in Genesis 3:15 is literal, so also is the seed of the serpent literal (to whatever degree). Advocates of a literal fulfillment of Genesis 3:15 say, *If the Devil is capable of injecting himself into humanity as the "seed of the serpent," why would it be so hard to believe that the fallen angels in some way did likewise cohabit with women?* Satan has repeatedly made bold attempts to pollute the bloodline of Christ in order to defeat the eternal purpose of God. It certainly appears valid that he actually attempted to literally pollute the bloodline of Christ through the "daughters of men" by the fallen "sons of God" (fallen angels).

80

In *Genesis 3:15,* we have the introduction of the first time in Scriptures that REDEMPTION would come through the same channel which DISOBEDIENCE was introduced in the human race, namely, **through the woman**. Also, it says the redeemer would be virgin born, or **seed of woman**, not man. This verse also tells us that **the Redeemer** will eventually deliver a deathblow to Satan, **"He (Jesus) shall bruise thy head."**

The great scheme is that Satan attempts to cut off, corrupt, and taint the offspring of Eve's bloodline (seed of the woman). Satan had many plots:

➢ Cain murdered his brother

➢ The fallen angels and demons attempted to corrupt the bloodline

➢ Abraham's wife was barren and past age

➢ The attempted destruction of chosen family (Genesis 50:20)

➢ Pharaoh's attempt to exterminate the Jewish male line and Moses the deliverer of

Israel (Exodus chapters 1 and 2).

➢ Haman's attempt to destroy all the Jews (Esther 3:8-9)

➢ Herod's attempt to destroy the Christ-child (Matthew 2:13-16)

➢ The devil even tempted (tested) Jesus (Matthew 4:1-10).

Note: Jesus could only be tempted or tested **outwardly** of sin. He could not be tempted **inwardly** because there was no sin in Him; He knew no sin.

Satan continued to attempt to thwart God's eternal purpose even after Jesus defeated him at the Cross of Calvary:

> Hitler's attempt to destroy the Jews (even experimenting with the genome of man)

> Islam attempts to destroy the Jews. Muslims presently rain down thousands of rockets upon Israel yearly.

> Today (2012), all major nations (nearly) are aligned against the Jew except America and under the present Obama administration, America is also. (Note: since this initial writing, America has elected a pro-Israel president.)

> Antichrist's attempt to destroy the Jews (future time in The Great Tribulation)

The part of Genesis 3:15 in which everybody is compliant is the "seed of the woman" which speaks prophetically of **Messiah Jesus**.

Genesis 3:15: And I will put enmity between thee and the woman, and between **thy seed** (the serpent's; Satan's seed) and **her seed** (the woman's seed; Eve's; Mary's**); it** (the seed of the woman; Christ) **shall bruise thy head**, and thou shalt bruise his heel.

Seed of the Serpent

That only leaves the controversial part "seed of the serpent" to be rightly interpreted.

It appears to this writer that there are several "possible" interpretations for the meaning of the "seed of the serpent:"

a.) (?) "Seed of the serpent" is literal prophecy even as the "seed of the woman" is literal prophecy and supports the **theory** that the "sons of God" in Genesis 6 were fallen angels, that in some fashion (possession of men's bodies ?), cohabited with earth women. There are those that suppose that Daniel 2:43 may support the mingling of the seed of fallen angels with the seed of men. Perhaps this corrupted seed could alter the genome of men and produce giants.

b.) (?) "Seed of the serpent" is only figurative and refers to wicked followers of Satan

c.) (?) "Seed of the serpent" speaks of **total demonic possession**, as in Judas Iscariot and the demon possessed man of the country of Gadara. Of course, others were also possessed of devils. Even this version may be interpreted "literally" as the seed of the serpent.

(Note: Some think that Judas Iscariot will be re-incarnated as the Antichrist)

d.) (?) "Seed of the serpent" is not properly interpreted by anyone as yet.

e.) (?) "Seed of the serpent" is a literal prophecy concerning the coming Antichrist.

The writer's own interpretation agrees with the probability of a demon or even Satan entering into and totally possessing a man who conjugates with a harlot-woman to produce a totally satanic person, the Antichrist; this appears to be reasonable and congruent with Genesis 3:15. This opinion is synonymous with a literal interpretation of both parts of the Genesis 3:15 prophecy.

Although there are three evil entities prominent in the book of Revelation, the reader must keep in mind that two of the three evil entities are in human form. This evil duo is paired together in Revelation chapter 13, the political **beast** (Antichrist) **out of the sea** (people; nations; Mediterranean

Sea) and the religious **beast out of the earth** (the false prophet and minister of the One-World apostate false religion which is the Bride of Antichrist). These two evil entities are mentioned together in Revelation 13:1-15; 16:13; 19:20; 20:10.

Again, the writer would be remiss if he did not make it clear that he is not convinced that a *fallen* angel could literally cohabit sexually with an earth woman. This is in spite of "unfallen" angels transforming themselves into the form of a man.

Satan's Hatred

The hatred of Satan toward God and God's people will reach its zenith in that awful day yet to come, commonly referred to as, THE TRIBULATION (Daniel's 70th Week of Daniel 9:24-27). This time of judgment is also called, "The Time of Jacob's Trouble" (Jeremiah 30:7).

It is estimated that over 50 million Christians were murdered during the Dark Ages (Medieval Age; Middle Ages - 600-1500 AD). These religious atrocities were authorized under the counterfeit guise of orthodox religion which was veiled and tolerated under the color of law. We know that many more saints of God will bathe the earth with their blood (radical Muslims daily murder Christians, Jews, and non-Muslims around the world as well as their own kind). But we equally know that every martyred saint shall resurrect in bodies made anew from their musty graves in glorious and eternal triumph. **Because He lives, we shall live also.**

Satan will be locked up for the one-thousand-year Millennial Rule of Christ and then released afterwards for a short season to wage war. Afterwards Satan will be consigned forever to the lake of fire (Revelation 20:10).

84

Addendum to the Sons of God and Daughters of Men by Dr. Henry M. Morris:

(*The Defenders Study Bible*, p. 32, World Publishing)

Genesis 6:2: That the sons of God saw the daughters of men that they were fair; and they took them wives of all which they chose.

Sons of God

Dr. Henry Morris says, "The identity of these 'sons of God' has been a matter of much discussion, but the obvious meaning is that they were angelic beings. This was the uniform interpretation of the ancient Jews, who translated the phrase as 'angels of God' in their Septuagint translation of the Old Testament. The apocryphal books of Enoch elaborate this interpretation, which is also strongly implied by the New Testament passages (I Peter 3:19-20; 2 Peter 2:4-6; Jude 6). The Hebrew phrase is *bene elohim*, which occurs elsewhere only in Job 1:6; 2:1; 38:7. In these three explicitly parallel usages, the contextual meaning can be nothing except that of angels. A similar phrase *bar elohim*, occurs in Daniel 3:25, and another *bar elim*, occurs in Psalm 29:1 and Psalm 89:6. All of these also refer explicitly to angels. The intent of the writer of Genesis 6 (probably Noah) was clearly that of introducing a monstrous irruption (*burst suddenly or violently; increase abruptly in size of population*) of demonic forces on the earth, leading to universal corruption and eventual judgment."

(NOTE: The writer believes that Moses wrote Genesis 6, not Noah. Neither does the writer put a lot of trust in the un-inspired apocryphal books of Enoch and other extra-biblical books, even though they may contain some factual historical material.)

Sons of God...Took Them Wives

85

Dr. Morrison says the "taking" of these women most likely refers to fallen angels, or demons, "possessing" their bodies. The word "wives" (Hebrew *ishshah*) is better translated "women. "There is no necessary intimation of actual marriage involved. By this time sin history, anarchism and amorality were so widespread that these demons were easily able to take possession of the bodies of multitudes of ungodly men; these in turn engaged in promiscuous sex with demon-possessed women, with a resulting rapid population growth, Satan perhaps hoping thereby to generate a vast army of human recruits to his rebellion and also to thwart the coming of God's promised Seed by thus corrupting all flesh.

The Sons of God and Noah's ark

The writer cannot endorse the opinion of "a godly line of Seth marrying into a wicked line of Cain" for the following obvious reason: If this "so-called" godly line was the descendants of Seth (Genesis 4:26; 5:6-24), they would have been included among those entering the ark that Noah built. Both of the alleged godly line of Seth and ungodly line of Enoch are in the same chronological time frame as Noah's ark. This period of time is just before the earth's judgment of the world-wide flood. The reason for the flood was because of the wide-spread wickedness of man and only eight people were deemed worthy of saving by God. Leviticus 18:23 and other passages suggest that mankind was guilty of bestiality (sexual relations between humans and animals). Consequently, there was no godly line of Seth right before the flood; there was only" just" Noah and his immediate family that were godly and God may have spared them for ten righteous just as He would have spared Sodom and Gomorrah if there had been ten righteous (Genesis 18:32). If eight people of Noah's family were righteous enough to be saved, then perhaps God would have spared the world from the great universal deluge for only a few more righteous souls. If a godly line of Seth existed at this time before the flood, surely their righteous lineage would have contributed to more than a small required quorum to avert God's judgment. Noah's ark would have had far many more than eight people aboard if there had existed a godly line of Seth or Enoch..

Recapping Reasons for Rejecting an Ungodly line of Canaan Marrying into a Godly Line of Seth

If the seed of the woman in Genesis 3:15 is a literal prophecy, then **so is** the seed of the serpent of the same verse also a literal prophecy. The writer does not believe that part of the verse of Genesis 3:15 is literal and the other part of the same verse is figurative. The writer believes that both parts of the prophecy of Genesis 3:15 are synonymous in meaning and both literal in fulfillment. Both the seed of the woman and the seed of the serpent must be taken as literal prophecies, else the verse is incongruous (lacking in harmony or agreement; incompatible; not proper or reasonable). This fact alone does not support a godly line of Seth marrying an ungodly line of Cain, but it does open the door for some form of fallen angelic contamination of mankind.

a. An 'ungodly line of Cain marrying into a godly line of Seth" militates against a form of satanic, supernatural intrusion into the blood line and genome of humanity.

b. The sons of God in Job 38:4-7 were **angels present at Creation** when God laid the foundations of earth. Why are sons of God in Job 38:7 different from sons of God in Genesis chapter 6?Again, the fact that the sons of God are angels does not favor the interpretation of them as a "godly line of Seth."

c. If there was a godly line of believers before Noah's flood, why were they absent when Noah was "long time" (maybe 120 years or much longer) building the ark? Why were some of them not in the ark with Noah?

d. Why would the unequal yoke of the marriage of believers with unbelievers cause men of renown, of superior mental faculties? It would appear that an unequal yoke of a godly line with an ungodly line would tend to produce men with less mental finesse (perhaps a mutation) than superior mentality. Instead, a yoke of angelic demon possessed men with daughters of men would appear to favor some kind of supernatural forces affecting the human genome to produce giant offspring. It does not make sense that the marriage of an ungodly line would enhance or improve a race of men of renown (of greater intelligence) as some of our intellectual brethren interpret. Demonic possession of humans could affect the genome in some physiological way as to produce giants in stature.

e. To avoid confusion on the interpretation of Genesis 6:2, why didn't the Scriptures expressly state that a godly line of Seth took wives of the ungodly line of Canaan? Of course, that could be implied, but there is no biblical or historical proof to substantiate it.

f. There is a tendency among believers **to rule out the supernatural intervention** of angels and relegate everything to the natural order of human experience. Satan himself walketh about seeking whom he may devour (I Peter 5:8) and while he is about it, he is transformed into an angel of light (2 Corinthians 11:14). Therefore, it is no great thing if his ministers also be transformed as the ministers of righteousness (2 Corinthians 11:15).

g. Actually, we wrestle not against flesh and blood, but against principalities, against powers, against the rulers of the darkness of this world, against **spiritual wickedness in high places** (Ephesians 6:12). Satan has a very large entourage of demons at his disposal.

The Word of God Greater Than All

While the writer thrills at the thought of just seeing an angel (after all, God created and ordained them), he is quick to remember that not even the angels take precedence over **God's Word, the Holy Bible**. God honors His Word above His name (Psalms 138:2).

God preserved His Word and English speaking people have a faithful translation in the **Authorized 1611 King James Version**.

God Preserved Word Takes Precedence

*Psalms 12:6-7: **The Words of the LORD** are pure words: as silver tried in a furnace of earth, purified seven times. Thou shalt **keep them**, O Lord thou shalt **preserve them** from this generation **for ever**.*

*Psalms 119:89: **For ever**, O LORD, **Thy Word** is **settled** in heaven.*

*Isaiah 40:8: The grass withereth, the flower fadeth: but **the Word of our God** shall **stand for ever**.*

*Matthew 24:35: Heaven and earth shall pass away, but My **Words shall not pass away**.*

*I Peter 1:25: But **the Word of the Lord endureth for ever**. And this is **the Word** which by the Gospel is preached unto you.*

Also see Psalms 78:1-8; 105:8; 119:111, 152, 160; Proverbs 22:20-21; Ecclesiastes 3:14; Isaiah 30:8; 59:21; Matthew 4:4; John 12:49-50; 17:8; I Peter 1:23.

Psalms 118:8: It is better to trust in the Lord that to put confidence in man.

And the God of peace shall yet bruise Satan under your feet shortly (Romans 16:20)

God promised to preserved His original inspired Word which we have in faithful copies of copies of copies; He did not promise to preserve the original scrolls, vellum, and papyrus that it was written upon.

Saints Will Observe, Interact and Dwell With Angels

*John 3:3: Jesus answered and said unto him, Verily, verily, I say unto thee, Except a man be **born again**, he cannot **see** the kingdom of God (I Corinthians 6:3)*

Angels will be bodily (celestial) and visibly present in the Kingdom during the Millennial Reign of Christ upon earth. Angels will be present in Heaven with the Lord and to be absent from the body is to be present with the Lord.

The sight of angels will pale compared to the sight of our Lord Jesus.

*Titus 3:5: **Not by works of righteousness** which we have done, but according to his mercy he saved us, by the washing of regeneration, and renewing of the Holy Ghost.*

Saints will be washed clean by Christ's blood (Revelation 1:5) and renewed by the Holy Ghost. They will be part of the Millennial Kingdom that consists of both redeemed men and angels.

*Ephesians 2:8-9: For by grace are ye saved **through faith**; and that not of yourselves: **it is the gift of God**: Not of works, lest any man should boast.*

90

Salvation is a must to inherit the kingdom of God.

*Romans 10:9-10, 13: That if thou shalt confess with thy mouth the Lord Jesus, and shalt **believe in thine heart** that God hath raised Him from the dead, thou shalt be saved. For with the heart man believeth unto righteousness; and with the mouth confession is made unto salvation. For whosoever shall call upon the name of Lord shall be saved.*

Salvation guarantees the saved that they will see the angels of God, however the sight of God the Father and the Lamb of God will be far greater.

It is not clearly revealed if the unsaved will either mingle or **see** the fallen angels **in** Hell. That scene will be one of **outer darkness** (Matthew 8:12; 22:13; 25:30). However, *"those which do iniquity shall be cast into a furnace of fire by the good angels* (Matthew 13:41-42; 25:41).

<u>Seeing the face of God and his Son is far greater than seeing an angel</u>

*Matthew 18:10: Take heed that ye despise not one of these little ones; for I say unto you, That in heaven their **angels do always behold the face of my Father** which is in heaven. For the Son of man is come to save that which was lost.*

*Psalm 17:15: As for me, **I will behold thy face in righteousness**: I shall be satisfied, when I awake, with thy likeness.*

*Psalm 84:9: Behold, O God our shield, and **look upon the face of thine anointed.** For a day in thy courts is better than a thousand. I had rather be a doorkeeper in the house of* *my God, than to dwell in the tents of wickedness.*

*I Corinthians 13:12: For now we see through a glass darkly; **but then face to face**: now I know in part; but then shall I know even as also I am known.*

The writer marvels at the supernatural greatness of angels particularly because they are a special creation of God Himself, even attending to His throne. There is no doubt that many have seen angels unaware and perhaps even the reader of this paper. Be mindful that Part II of this paper is largely the writer's speculation concerning the identity of the sons of God in Genesis chapter 6. The writer welcomes the interpretations and opinions of those opposed to his. After all, this subject does not concern salvation.

(Disclaimer: Concerning this brief article, the writer has not made an attempt at thoroughly examining the nature of angels and their deeds. It is certain that the writer makes no claim of being an authority concerning angels other than what is expressly stated in Scriptures.

For Christians that are "babes in Christ," this writing may be too profound at first reading. A tender plant newly placed in soft soil, can be washed out of the ground with strong currents of waters (strong meat does not belong to babes) even as a newborn baby cannot properly digest solid food. *"Strong meat belongeth to them that are of full age"* [mature Christians] – Hebrews 5:11-14.As Peter says in 2 Peter 3:16,: *"...in which some things hard to be understood.*)

Why this Writing on Angels

Because angels are such a fascinating subject, the writer thought to gather some interesting facts from the Bible that perhaps others have not had time to delve into. Too, the writer wanted to query some puzzling questions concerning the meaning of the "sons of God" in an effort to stimulate interest in Biblical study.

*Malachi 3:16: Then they that feared the LORD spake often one to another: and the LORD hearkened, and heard it, and a book of remembrance was written before him for them that feared the LORD, and **that thought upon his name**.*

ABOUT THE AUTHOR

The writer was born in Greenville, SC in 1934 and was a lifetime resident except for two years in the US Army (Fort Jackson, S.C. and Fort Carson, Colorado) and two years residence in Florida.

After separation (honorably) from the US Army, the writer returned to Greenville, SC and married at age 27 to Christine Moore, an old acquaintance from an adjacent neighborhood. The Lord blessed us with six daughters, Debbie, Donna, Dale, Denise, Deree, and Dena.

A short time after marriage, the writer was convicted of his lost condition as a sinner and after a miserable time under conviction the writer confessed his sin and lost condition to God and was saved.

The writer was 40 years of age when he began attending college (3 years, no diploma).

The writer retired as a chemical technologist from Morton International Chemical Company in 1996. Before retirement, the writer had the urge to write on Bible subjects and wished that he had more time to study. Upon retirement, the writer bought a computer and became a novice writer.

The writer now resides in Easley, S.C.

D. Helton has written several documents and books, as well as the books or booklets: "Jesus is God," "Evolution, Another False Religion of Humanism," "Cremation: Christian or Pagan," "Is The Gap Theory Credible?" "Does Water Baptism Save," "Can a Saved Person Become Unsaved," and several others, available here:

http://www.theoldpathspublications.com/Pages/Authors/Helton.htm#God

Brother Helton may be contacted here:

Dennis D. Helton
200 Home Place Drive
Easley, SC 29640

www.ingramcontent.com/pod-product-compliance
Lightning Source LLC
Chambersburg PA
CBHW072012060426
42446CB00042B/2301